PASTORAL MINISTRY FROM A COVENANTAL

PERSPECTIVE:

WITH SPECIFIC APPLICATION TO THE RCUS

Maynard A. Koerner

Printed in the United States of America

To my dear wife, Marcia, the love of my life, whose encouragement and patience is deeply appreciated. Also to my children, their spouses and grandchildren. I pray that their faith in God would continue through the generations.

CONTENTS

APPENDIX

1

INTRODUCTION

Statement of Concern

God promises in Ezekiel 34 that He will provide a shepherd for His sheep. This is ultimately pointing to the Son of God who is the Savior of God's people, the Church. The picture of the Savior as the shepherd and the Church as the sheep is an important concept throughout the Scriptures. There is no greater demonstration of this than in Psalm 23. Psalm 23 presents a picture of what it means to be the people of God and to have Him as our God. The people of God are compared to sheep, and the Savior is the shepherd. The implication is that God's people benefit by having the Lord as a shepherd in the same manner as sheep do. It also implies that God does care for His people and provides for their needs. It is the quintessential picture of pastoral care. This is emphasized in the grammar and use of the word shepherd.

> That service is described in the urgent call to "shepherd the flock of God among you." The verb "shepherd" (Greek, *poimaino*) is in the emphatic position and the imperative mood indicating that shepherding the flock is the essential work of the elder according to Peter. "There is no word in the whole round of primitive ecclesiastical phraseology which is more frequently used to express the relation of office-bearer than 'to shepherd'" (Witmer, 2010, p. 35).

Another classic passage which presents the idea of a shepherd caring for and feeding the sheep is in the good shepherd

11

passage of John 10. Here again Jesus is the shepherd who calls and gathers His sheep and who cares for them. The ultimate benefit of having this care is that all of the sheep will be gathered and not one of them will be lost. Again we see the reality and the importance of the pastoral nature of the relationship between God and His people. The concept is repeated in John 21, where Jesus tells Peter three times to feed His sheep.

The concepts embedded in the words "shepherd," "sheep," "care" and "feeding" demonstrate the notion that God's people are a people who need care, and that God provides that care. This nourishment is generally spoken of as pastoral ministry. The word "ministry" implies service and the word "pastoral" defines the type of service. However, one must not assume that everything which is done in the Church today under the formal title of "ministry" is truly service, or that it is pastoral in nature. I do not believe that the Church of Christ is truly served if those who lead the Church are not truly ministering and are not doing so in a pastoral way.

I believe everything that properly comes under the heading of ministry is pastoral. However, it appears to me there is a real tension in ministry today. The tension in ministry is between that which is seen as doctrinal and a ministry of proclamation, and that which is seen as practical and a ministry of care. In my opinion this tension can be seen even in the way that seminaries--in particular independent seminaries--seek to present their curriculum. Some seminaries tend to present themselves as having a strong doctrinal emphasis and some present themselves with more of an emphasis on the practical.

This tension is not necessary and ministry should first of all be understood as pastoral. To understand ministry in this way does not take anything away from the importance of being doctrinal and the necessity of being practical. But it does recognize that central to ministry, with ministry being defined as meeting the needs of God's people, is the idea of Jesus as the Great Shepherd who leads His sheep to pasture.

There is a need today for ministers of the gospel to have a deeper appreciation and understanding of the pastoral nature of ministry. This would have a great effect in the application of ministry in the Church. It is also my contention that the concept of pastoral ministry is rooted in the peculiar relationship which God has established with His people. Scripture presents this relationship in terms of a covenant. It is my intention to demonstrate that the theological understanding of God as a covenant God relates to how we understand pastoral ministry. This theological understanding assists us in thinking about the way God looks upon His people as He establishes them, and how He sees them in His ongoing relationship with them. A keen awareness of the needs of the people whom God calls to Himself informs us of their ongoing needs.

There is a great description of the care that Christ, the Great Shepherd, gives to the Church in Ephesians 5:25-27:

> Husbands, love your wives, as Christ loved the church and gave himself up for her, that he might sanctify her, having cleansed her by the washing of water with the word, so that he might present the church to himself in splendor, without spot or wrinkle or any such thing, that she might be holy and without blemish.

This is what God has promised in His covenant. It is fulfilled through His Son, our Lord. It is this service to God which ministers of the gospel are called to. Therefore, my concern that all ministry should be seen as pastoral in nature is rooted in the teaching of Scripture as it is understood from the reformed, covenantal perspective.

Background for this Study

This conviction and concern "that all ministry should be seen as pastoral," is something which I have arrived at as a result of having served in the capacity of pastoral ministry for over thirty-four years. My experience comes from having served as a minister of the gospel in the Reformed Church in the United States (RCUS). I have also been a member of the RCUS all of my life, and so has my family for as many generations as I am aware of. This is a denomination whose history goes back to the 16th century German Reformation. The RCUS was founded in 1725 as a German immigrant church in Pennsylvania by the Rev. John Philip Boehm (rcus.org). The RCUS struggled with liberalism already in the latter half of the 1800's, leading to a merger with a non-reformed church in 1934 which became the Evangelical and Reformed Church (The Reformed Church, 1975). At that time one classis, the Eureka Classis existing in the Dakotas, determined to continue the RCUS.

This was a small, struggling denomination for many years. The RCUS today has four classes, with a general synod. It remains a fairly small denomination with 45-50 congregations primarily existing in the Midwest and western United States, with a handful of congregations in the eastern part of the United States (RCUS Abstract, 2013).

While holding to the German reformed heritage is quite important, the RCUS has moved on from being simply a German immigrant church. The creeds of the RCUS are the Three Forms of Unity consisting of the Heidelberg Catechism, the Belgic Confession, and the Canons of Dort (RCUS Constitution, 1997). There is particular emphasis on using the Heidelberg Catechism as a means for the members to know and express their faith. This reformation creed is a very personal expression of the biblical faith with particular emphasis upon the established relationship with God.

The RCUS strongly emphasizes the importance of catechizing the youth. This catechetical instruction includes the memorization of the questions and answers which make up the Heidelberg Catechism (RCUS Constitution, 1997). Upon completing the process of catechizing the covenant youth are received into communicant membership of the Church by the rite of confirmation.

In seeking to move beyond being strictly an ethnic church and to obey the word of God, the RCUS has had a strong emphasis upon missions. This has led to many of the congregations being fairly small, since they are recent church plants. Also the older, long established congregations are not overly large. Ministry in the RCUS consists almost exclusively of one minister in each congregation, carrying out all of the aspects of ministry in conjunction with the church elders.

With some exceptions, the work of ministry in the RCUS involves providing for all of the pastoral needs of the members. It is also a ministry which requires an understanding of and a familiarity with the particular heritage and emphasis which exists within the RCUS. Being a small denomination, the RCUS has often had to rely on finding pastors who have not grown up within the denomination. This can lead to some struggles for pastors and congregations.

It is out of my personal and pastoral experience within the context of the RCUS, as well as the interest I have in developing a full understanding of ministry as it is understood from a covenantal context, that leads me to pursue this study. It is my prayer that it will be helpful to pastors and beneficial to the Church of Jesus Christ.

Theological Understanding which will Guide this Study

I believe that approaching pastoral ministry from a covenantal perspective is also important in light of the present emphasis which one finds in what has been called "evangelical Christianity." David F. Wells in his book The Courage to Be Protestant (2008), has done an excellent job in documenting recent developments in evangelicalism. This development has been greatly influenced by an over-emphasis upon the individual and his personal relationship with God. Wells points this out in the following statement:

> But the largest factor in this internal change, I think, was that evangelicalism began to be infested by the culture in which it was living. And then

15

> Christianity became increasingly reduced simply to
> private, internal, therapeutic experience. Its
> doctrinal form atrophied and then crumbled (p. 8).

My concern in regard to this emphasis is how it has
affected what "church" is, and therefore the pastoral ministry of
the Church. Again I turn to Wells (2008) and his description of
what effect this emphasis has had on the Church. He finds that
within this development the attitude became one of disconnect
with the Church. He then goes on to say:

> Previously the churches had been a focal point for
> Christian believers, now they lost that place. As
> unlikely as it seems, many churches in a sense
> disappeared. They became entirely parachurch in
> nature!
>
> The leaders of this marketing enterprise
> understood that they were in a market, and religious
> customers had choices. The choices that began to
> be offered by way of competition, however, were all
> along the lines of not being churchy. This new
> direction was mightily reinforced by the emergence
> of the television ministries, especially in the 1980s,
> not to mention the pervasive availability of religious
> videos. Church life subsided in importance for
> many people, if only because on Sunday morning
> they could, and often did, "go to church" in their
> living rooms in front of their television sets. One
> whole segment of the evangelical world decided to
> practice Christian faith as if the whole notion of the
> church needed to disappear. Evangelicalism was
> becoming *para* in mentality, and the local church
> was about to become its chief casualty (p. 11).

If the church has become a casualty, then the pastoral
ministry of the church has also become a casualty. My desire is to
see how pastoral ministry is rooted in a true biblical understanding
of the Church. The doctrinal commitment which is present in the
reformed church provides a theological basis for maintaining

pastoral care of the Church. The emphasis upon the covenantal relationship provides this basis.

Covenant theology understands that the believer does have a personal relationship with Christ, but it is understood in the context of the covenant community. The covenant community is made up of those called out by God for the purpose of being His special people. The relationship within this covenant community is formalized by means of believers uniting themselves together as a congregation under the spiritual oversight of elders and pastor. The individuals who make up this community are in need of ongoing care and maintenance as the people of God. This care is provided through the Church both by mutual fellowship with and encouragement of fellow members, and by means of the offices of pastor, elder, and deacon. It seems evident that the purpose of the Church is implied in the covenantal structure which is the means by which God seeks to establish His people.

It is this covenantal structure which serves as the basis for establishing an approach to pastoral ministry. This approach to ministry is also rooted in one of the great creeds of the Church, the Heidelberg Catechism. In my estimation there is no better, succinct statement of the biblical faith than that contained in Question and Answer #1 of the Heidelberg Catechism:

> What is your only comfort in life and in death?

> That I, with body and soul, both in life and in death, am not my own, but belong to my faithful Savior Jesus Christ, who with His precious blood has fully satisfied for all my sins, and redeemed me from all the power of the devil; and so preserves me that without the will of my Father in heaven not a hair can fall from my head; indeed, that all things must work together for my salvation. Wherefore, by His Holy Spirit He also assures me of eternal life, and makes me heartily willing and ready from now on to live unto Him (The Three Forms, 2006 p. 3).

The emphasis here is on the idea of belonging to God by means of the accomplished work of Christ. This is again a covenantal notion. There are a number of important implications here. Not only is the comfort of the believer based on God's initiative and His provision of the Savior, it is also based on the established relationship with Christ which is expressed by public confession and membership in the Church. There are a number of implications for understanding ministry here.

First, is the notion of belonging to Jesus Christ. The pastor, who is called to provide care for the believer, is providing care for someone who is the possession of the Lord Jesus Christ. This is an established relationship. It is established by Christ. It is not held out as a possibility for those confessing Christ, it is a reality. The work of ministry then must be focused on being the caretakers of those who are the possession of Christ.

Second, is the importance of looking at the finished work of Christ. There is an important emphasis upon the effectual nature of the priestly work of Christ. Again the comfort of the believer is based solidly on what has been accomplished for him. To understand this work of Christ and to grasp the implication of the effect of His work, is to have comfort. The answer which must be provided for the child of God concerning his sin is assurance that the problem of sin has been taken care of.

Third, is the understanding of responding to this accomplished relationship. The life of the believer is one of responding to God's work of grace. The believer comes to understand that, based on implications one and two above, he is ready to serve His Savior. What a comforting thought that the life we live is not one of seeking to measure up, but one of belonging and now enjoying that relationship. Again this informs and guides the pastor to a great extent in his approach to ministry.

What the authors of the Heidelberg Catechism captured here is covenantal theology and they have applied it in a very personal and meaningful way to the concept of what the Church of Christ is all about. A colleague of mine once stated that what is unique about the Heidelberg Catechism is that it has captured in its statement of faith the personal relationship which the believer has with God (C.W. Powell, personal communication, summer 2008). I would add that this personal faith is solidly rooted in the covenantal relationship which God has established. I am convinced this historic reformed creed serves as a great handbook for pastoral ministry as well as a learning tool and a confessional statement.

In the reformed confession, the Heidelberg Catechism, the believer is assured that he can trust God. His trust is not only that God is true, but that God will guide and lead him in every step of his life.

> Someone well said that one of the most inspiring of truths is that God has a distinct plan for each one of us in sending us into this world. This plan embraces not only His original creation of us, but also the family and social setting into which we were born. It includes all the vicissitudes of life, all the seemingly chance or random happenings, and all the sudden and unexpected turn of events, both 'good' and 'bad,' that occur in our lives. All these situations and circumstances, though they may appear only as happenstance to us, were written in God's book before one of them came to be (Bridges, 1988, p. 165).

Knowing that this is what the covenant relationship between God and His people is all about only serves to underscore the need to understand the role of the minister. As the members of the Church go through life, and the various struggles of life, God has provided the minister as a means to keep them in His care.

The basis for this concept is clearly established in Scripture. Much of the same language is used by the Apostle Paul as he addresses the Ephesian elders in Acts 20:28: "Pay careful attention to yourselves and to all the flock, in which the Holy Spirit has made you overseers, to care for the Church of God, which he obtained with his own blood." The Church belongs to God; He has purchased it. The means by which the purchase has been made is by the blood of Christ. Having purchased the Church with His blood indicates that the Church is very precious to Christ. He has great concern that this precious possession is provided for, and He establishes the means for this provision in the office of pastor/elder.

This statement in Acts 20:28 is made in the context of instructing the overseers, pastors/elders, concerning their task of caring for the Church. The fact is that the Church which they are to care for is God's possession. It has been purchased and it fully belongs to Him. Christ is the Shepherd and Head of His Church. The one who carries out pastoral ministry is to be a steward. They have been entrusted with the care of the sheep which are the possession of God, paid for by the blood of Christ.

There is a close connection with the covenantal relationship of God and His Church. It is also the case that, in being this special possession, the foundation is established for the Church to carry out its purpose and function. In the context of describing the Church and its function we read this in I Peter 2:9: "But you are a chosen race, a royal priesthood, a holy nation, a people for His own possession, that you may proclaim the excellencies of Him who called you out of darkness into His marvelous light." Notice the reference to God's own possession for the purpose of proclaiming His excellencies. Thus believers belong to God in terms of their very identity. They also then carry out the function of serving Him by making known who He is. There is again an important direction here in terms of ministry. Ministry is to assist the people in comprehending who they are and how they can make known who God is as they live their lives.

The notion that the people of God are portrayed in Scripture as His flock or His sheep, is equally important. We learn a great deal about the people of God in comparing them to sheep. Jesus Himself speaks in John 10 of being the Good Shepherd and knowing His flock. The means by which the shepherd provides for the sheep is pictured in a wonderful way in Psalm 23. This picture of sheep and their shepherd provides two important implications for ministry. First of all, sheep are very stubborn animals. They get into trouble very easily. Secondly, they need constant care as they cannot care for themselves.

God has gathered unto Himself a people who are far from perfect. They are His special possession. This possession is precious and important to Him. That does not mean that there are no problems or shortcomings with God's people. They stand before God based on what Christ has done for them, while they are still weak and covered with blemishes. I have a real concern that ministry must not be seen as preparing people to be without blemish so that they can be the people of God. Rather, it is to recognize that they, the people of God, have blemishes and require pastoral ministry to assist them in dealing with these blemishes. It is Christ as the head and groom of the Church who provides for the bride that she might be "without spot and wrinkle" (Eph. 5:27). Then it is through the pastoral ministry of the Church that the implications of having been cleansed by the blood of Christ are experienced.

We have thus far noted the implications for ministry from the perspective of understanding what the Church is. It now remains to see the implications for ministry based on this concept of the Church. In the quote given above from the Heidelberg Catechism, the implications for the believer based on the covenantal relationship are clearly stated: "makes me heartily willing and ready from now on to live unto Him" (The Three Forms, 2001). The people of God are called out of darkness into the marvelous light of Christ so that they might give their lives as a thanksgiving in service to God (Rom. 12:1). Such a life of obedience before God is only possible by the enabling strength of the Holy Spirit. The Spirit works through the Word.

Understanding the Extent of Pastoral Ministry

I have sought to establish that the Church is the possession of God, and that this possession is precious to God. Also, He has given the Great Shepherd--His Son--for the sake of the sheep. Jesus, who is the Great Shepherd, did not forsake the sheep when

He finished His work on earth and ascended into heaven. Jesus makes it clear to His disciples that the Comforter would be sent and would be with them. The Holy Spirit was poured out on the Church on the day of Pentecost. The New Testament Church has a great advantage in being indwelled with the Holy Spirit.

The implications of understanding this relationship from a covenantal perspective are far reaching. While simply being God's covenant people has far reaching implications, it is not just a static relationship. The picture of Christ as the Great Shepherd is one of providing ongoing care for the flock. What is this care and how does it take place? This study will seek to explore not only the covenantal implications for ministry, but also examine various aspects of that ministry itself. I will be dealing with a number of specific areas where pastoral ministry is to take place in the Church. Some of the areas which are presented in this study are basic to biblical ministry, while others are somewhat unique to the RCUS within the broader context of the Christian church.

Christ commissioned the Apostles to be witnesses to Him beginning in Jerusalem, also including Samaria, and going to the ends of the earth, that is, Rome (Acts 1:8). The work of bearing witness, that is the Apostles laying the foundation with Christ as the cornerstone, is the basis upon which the Church is to be built (Eph. 2:19-20). The basic structure which is the Church was put in place as we find it recorded in the book of Acts. The Apostles were concerned with the ongoing work of building the Church by continuing on that foundation.

According to I Peter 2:4-5, the Church is a building of living stones. We might say that Christ is a master spiritual stone mason. As a shepherd appointed by Christ, the task of the preacher is to provide that which the living stone needs in order to be indeed alive. It then follows that all of ministry is pastoral. In speaking specifically of preaching, Jay Adams (1982) says, "the pastoral preacher must be prepared at each gathering of the saints to use the Word in some way in order to 'equip' them for their work of ministry" (p. 12).

Certainly biblical ministry must be ministry of the Word. Yet, ministry is more than preaching. Pastoral ministry does not set aside the Word, but is an extension of the Word. It is not a stretch at all to say that all of ministry with its various aspects is pastoral in nature. This has tremendous implications for ministry, which is where I will concentrate my efforts in this study. The specific emphasis will be upon understanding the pastoral nature of the various aspects of ministry, and exploring the approach which needs to be taken in the various disciplines of ministry. My focus, therefore, in this examination will be on pastoral ministry which is covenantal. It is my desire to present pastoral ministry from a biblical understanding of the covenant and to explore how it applies to the task of ministry. My particular application of the ministry will be within the context of the RCUS.

It will be necessary to expand on the concepts already stated concerning the pastoral nature of ministry. The intent is to come up with a working definition of pastoral ministry. With this definition in place it will be necessary to demonstrate the pastoral application to its various categories. As with any task, the basic understanding of the context in which one functions, and the purpose of the task itself, will greatly influence how one goes about seeking to accomplish that task. Unto that end I will seek to define the task of ministry.

While this study will concentrate primarily on the work of the office of minister of the Word, it would be a grave oversight to not connect the work of the minister of the Word with the work of the eldership, which is designated in the RCUS as the Spiritual Council. How the Spiritual Council is to be an integral part of the pastoral ministry will also be explored. Basically I will seek to show that the work of the elders is an extension of the work of the pastor. They cannot have conflicting purposes, but are part of the total shepherding provision for the sheep.

Purpose for this Study

The purpose for this study is to demonstrate the need to understand the pastoral nature of ministry. I will focus my attention in this study on covenantal ministry within the context of the RCUS. As I examine the approach to ministry in this study I will rely heavily upon my experience as a lifelong member as well as a pastor of the RCUS. In my opinion, this experience has helped to shape my understanding of pastoral ministry.

I am convinced that the relationship between pastor and congregation is completely unique. I state this based on my own experiences along with those which other pastors have related to me. I have also acted as advisor in an official capacity in a situation where a pastor was struggling with the relationship with his congregation.

Members look to their pastor to meet a need for them which cannot be met anywhere else. Members want to hold their pastor in high regard, yet they can be very critical. It appears that members either have a great love and respect for their pastor, or they have no respect for him at all. I have found it to be very helpful when a pastor truly knows his people and they know him. They respond when it is apparent that he is a real person. It is very helpful for the pastor to establish a relationship with the members so that they can trust that he will meet their needs. With the possible exception of a particular ministry to youth or perhaps the elderly in a sizable congregation, I believe that the model of one pastor who truly leads and feeds the flock for Christ best reflects the pastoral nature of ministry as well as the picture of ministry we see in the Bible.

At the same time a pastor does represent Christ to his congregation. It is important to understand and have a sense of the office which he holds. If the word of God is given for the purpose of not only bringing comfort and encouragement to the flock, but also to rebuke and correct as we read in II Tim. 3:16-17, then the pastor must be able to convey that authority of the word of God to the flock. The concern for ministry to be truly caring, that is, pastoral in nature, should not be seen as a move away from the authority of the church officers in their responsibility. This is perhaps another trend today which would be a threat to true biblical ministry. Tom Erich (2011) elaborates on this in his article Opinion and Commentary.

> Look for less focus on familiar forms of authority like the Bible and ecclesiastical tradition. Instead, Christianity 2.0 will move away from expertise-based systems and arguments over right opinion, and focus more on creating circles of friends seeking God's presence and help, both in daily life and in the world beyond personal experience. Bottom line: less intellectualism, more intuition.

Ministry that Leads to Strength by the Members

I have selected a number of areas which in my estimation particularly deal with the needs of ministry in the context of the RCUS. I am sure that there are additional areas in which the principles of pastoral ministry could be applied.

All ministry must, of course, be based on the word of God. The notion of pastoral ministry suggests the picture of sheep feeding in the pasture. The word of God is the food. The use of the word of God for the ministry in the Church is to be seen in terms of feeding the flock. Proclaiming the Word simply for the sake of proclaiming the Word fails to see God's ultimate purpose in the provision of His word. This study will pursue an understanding of the "feeding" aspect of the Word. There is within the word of God serious warning and condemnation concerning sin. Yet, I have a real concern that pastors do not use the Word simply for the purpose of condemning the unbeliever and putting a guilt trip upon the struggling believer, but to truly be the food of comfort which God's people are in need of.

How then are the sheep to be fed? The discipline of feeding the sheep is once again in the context of the covenantal relationship. It is important to understand that feeding the sheep with the Word is feeding with covenantal instruction.

A specific aspect of covenantal instruction, which has historically been very important in the context of the RCUS, is the catechetical instruction of the covenant youth. This important tool in ministry is often looked at in today's culture in a very negative way. The idea of serious learning has been replaced with the satisfying of felt needs. I find this a very troubling trend. It is my hope to show the benefits of serious catechetical training. The study will specifically examine the concept of catechetical instruction for the covenant youth. The methodology to be used for this important ministry will also be examined.

Central to the pastoral ministry of the Church of God is worship. Therefore, it will also be the purpose of this study to examine the pastoral aspect of worship. Particular emphasis will be placed on the preaching ministry. The basic purpose of preaching must also be pastoral. It is important that the pastoral concept of ministry be central in the pursuit of preaching. I find myself in general agreement with Adams (1982) in his introduction concerning the quality of preaching today. In addition, my concern is that preaching not just be an academic exercise in presenting detailed information, but that it also speaks with passion to the hearts of God's people.

In looking at the overall ministry of the Church, there is one aspect which, in my opinion, is not considered very important at all today, and also not understood very well in terms of how it is to be used. This is the aspect of ministry referred to as "church polity," or the government of the Church. This study will seek to examine the courts of the Church in terms of how they are to be viewed and function as part of the overall pastoral ministry of the Church. Pastors must not see the Church courts' oversight as an intrusion or hindrance, but rather as an important tool in the ministry's purpose of feeding the sheep. The members also need to have a better understanding of the assistance available to them through the courts of the Church, as they desire to be faithful to the Head of the Church.

Certainly there are other aspects of ministry which could be pursued. For the purpose of this study the above listed areas have been selected. Again, this study will seek to establish the understanding that pastors are called to pastoral ministry in a covenantal context. My intent is to offer some guidance in regard to carrying out this ministry.

The office of minister of the Word can be very rewarding and very difficult. I am concerned that pastors do not fall into the trap of approaching the office as a place from which to lord over the flock, or to be just a friend. It can be a fine line and difficult to stay on course. It is my prayer that this presentation can be useful. The bottom line must always be to care for the flock. May God grant a pastor's heart to all who seek to provide ministry to His flock.

In addition to ministers of the gospel, there is a need for all believers to understand the concept of spiritual care which the Lord has made provision for through the Church. May this study also provide a better understanding of the relationship of all believers to their Lord by means of the full ministry of the Church, ministers, elders and fellow members.

2

DEFINITION OF PASTORAL MINISTRY

The Need for Pastoral Emphasis in Ministry

The reformed faith, based on Scripture, emphasizes the fact that salvation is the finished work of Christ on the cross. God has chosen unto Himself a people who have been purchased by Christ so that they might be God's special possession. The biblical presentation of the ministry of the Church is very much based on this reality. God provides a means so that His people are cared for and so that their needs are met. God also provides that His people become increasingly conformed to His image. The purpose of this care is to both establish God's people and to provide for their daily spiritual sustenance so that they will remain His people.

Christ is, of course, the chief Shepherd by whom this church is established and kept as the possession of God. This church is spoken of as the bride of Christ, and He is the groom (Eph. 5:22-32). Christ gave Himself so that the Church would benefit from Him. We further see that Christ makes specific provision for this care by means of human shepherds who serve the chief Shepherd. Jesus the chief Shepherd provides for the needs of His sheep by means of these human shepherds. The notion of pastors being shepherds for the chief Shepherd is spoken of by the apostle Peter in his first letter:

> So I exhort the elders among you, as a fellow elder and a witness of the sufferings of Christ, as well as a partaker in the glory that is going to be revealed: shepherd the flock of God that is among you, exercising oversight, not under compulsion, but

willingly, as God would have you; not for shameful gain, but eagerly; not domineering over those in your charge, but being examples to the flock. And when the chief Shepherd appears, you will receive the unfading crown of glory (I Pet. 5:1-4).

The manner in which this work of being a shepherd is perceived and carried out has varied throughout the history of the Church. It is also evident that the manner in which one understands what the Church is and what its mission is, greatly influences how this work of ministry is perceived and carried out. This is demonstrated by two very popular contemporary concepts of what the Church is supposed to be.

The first is a concept which has been generally referred to as "the church growth movement." The strong emphasis today on church growth has a particular influence in this regard. From this perspective the ministry of the Church is very much perceived as being geared towards increasing the number of church members. This approach to ministry has an emphasis which leads to very little need for doctrine, and even the spiritual growth of the believer. There is a strong focus on presenting the gospel to the lost, often in a very shallow way. The success and purpose for ministry is defined by numerical growth. This is an example where a very specific agenda drives the type of ministry that is provided to the Church.

> Church Growth is a movement within evangelical Christianity which aims to develop methods to grow churches. Various church leaders have proposed different ways to grow churches. One prominent example is the seeker-sensitive approach, which aims to make churches more accessible and sensitive to the needs of spiritual seekers.
> (ask.com/What=Is+A+Seeker+Church, 2010)

Secondly, we can note that a specific understanding of doctrine can and does define ministry. A particular doctrine of salvation can have a powerful influence on the approach to ministry. The focus becomes one of constantly dealing with the

30

question of whether one is actually saved. This leads to a lack of assurance and a constant vigil on whether one is saved or not. Such a ministry will continuously challenge the individual who confesses Christ in regards to the genuineness of his confession. It is therefore difficult to get beyond that initial point and build up those who are truly the people of God into mature, faithful members of the kingdom of God.

The two examples referenced above are demonstrations of how the ministry of the Church is often agenda driven. The agenda becomes the driving force or the defining emphasis for the ministry of the Church. The Church itself is then defined by a particular agenda. However, Scripture should be allowed to define the Church for us. The proper agenda for ministry will develop naturally when the definition of the Church is based on Scripture.

The reformed understanding of what the Church is and its doctrine of salvation certainly informs the minister on how to approach his ministry to his congregation. In particular, seeing the covenantal relationship which God has established with His people is fundamental in understanding the role of the servant of Christ who is called to shepherd His flock. There are a number of implications that define what biblical ministry is, implications that come directly from the concept of the covenant.

God promised in Exodus 6:6-8 that He would establish the people of Israel as His people and He would be their God:

> Say therefore to the people of Israel, "I am the LORD, and I will bring you out from under the burdens of the Egyptians, and I will deliver you from slavery to them, and I will redeem you with an outstretched arm and with great acts of judgment. I will take you to be my people, and I will be your God, and you shall know that I am the LORD your God, who has brought you out from under the burdens of the Egyptians. I will bring you into the land that I swore to give to Abraham, to Isaac, and to Jacob. I will give it to you for a possession. I am the LORD."

31

This relationship is formally established when God renews the covenant at Mount Sinai in Exodus 19. We see this covenant formula repeated several times in the Old Testament and repeated in the New Testament in I Peter 2:9: "But you are a chosen race, a royal priesthood, a holy nation, a people for his own possession, that you may proclaim the excellencies of him who called you out of darkness into his marvelous light."

This covenant formula must be the basis for understanding pastoral ministry. It is a ministry of care for those who are the people of God. They are His precious possession. God described His covenant blessings while making the covenant in Exodus 19, when He reminded His people how He "bore them on eagles' wings." This is a God who cares for His people and who actually provides that which is needed so that His people remain in Him. He sent His Son to be the mediator by which His people are saved. It is this mediator who appoints shepherds to care for the flock in His name.

The Biblical Picture of the Church and the Task of the Shepherd

Drawing from Scripture a very simple definition for the Church is not an easy task; in fact the insistence on one simple definition has, in my opinion, at times led to distortions. We must determine from the context of Scripture the various characteristics and nuances of the word "church" as it is used in Scripture. A few words must be said regarding the biblical teaching concerning church from the specific perspective of its implications for ministry.

Bannerman (1869) presents two primary characteristics of the Church or as he has described it, "the Christian society" (p. 18). His first characteristic deals with the origin of the Church. "In the first place, the Church is a Divine institution, owing its origin not to man, but to Christ, and associated together not in consequence of human arrangement, but by Christ's appointment" (p. 18). Recognizing that the Church is divine and not human requires that we allow God to instruct us as to the ministry which is to be carried out in His church. Ministry cannot merely be determined by convenience or human approval.

The above mentioned characteristic also speaks to the relationship which necessarily exists among fellow believers. It is impossible for individuals to be joined to Christ simply as individuals. To be joined to Christ causes one to also be joined to fellow believers who are equally united to Christ by their faith. Bannerman (1869) goes on to say "In the second place I remark, the Church of Christ is a spiritual institution; or, in other words, in its primary character it is a spiritual instrumentality for working out the spiritual good of man" (p. 24).

Without doubt we must come to recognize that the Church is spiritual in nature. This is recognized not only in that the Church is God's church, but also that it is through the Church that the spiritual needs of its members are met. Believers are spiritual in nature and have spiritual needs. The Church is the instrument by which Christ provides for this need. This provision begins in a direct way in that Christ has sent the Holy Spirit to dwell in the hearts of believers. This spiritual need is also provided for in that Christ has appointed servants to minister to His flock.

Reformed ecclesiology speaks of the Church as both an organization and an organism. To speak of the Church as an organism is to again understand that the Church is in need of care and feeding. It is this pastoral care that both meets the needs of the Church and establishes it to be an effective influence in the world.

> The Church is first of all an organism, a living Body whose head is Christ, energized by the Holy Spirit. It is in this fellowship that believers serve and encourage one another to spiritual maturity (Eph. 4:1-16), and it is from this fellowship that they go into the world in Jesus' name (John 20:21; I Thess. 1:4-8) (Smallman, 2003, p. 22).

The Means Given for Meeting Spiritual Needs

The Church then is made up of a people whom God has called out of this world and with whom He has established a relationship based on the fact that the Church is His precious possession. We further understand that God has made provision for the Church to keep it and care for it. Thus as we use the word "pastoral," it is this care which we reference. Specifically it is in reference to the shepherd who cares for the sheep. The Bible presents the Church as sheep who are cared for by the Shepherd. In reality the Church has all that it needs in the provision accomplished by the work of Christ. In Him we have been given life and in Him we live. Yet, there is a very practical application of this in that Christ has provided for an ongoing ministry as a means by which the reality of the finished work of Christ is applied in the lives of God's people. Christ has given to His church a ministry through the special offices of the Church. We understand these to be that of minister of the Word, elder, and deacon (RCUS Constitution, 1997). While all of these offices are pastoral in nature, the aspect of pastoral ministry applies most directly to the office of minister of the Word. The work of the elders, which will be discussed in chapter 8, is a work of support to the work of the pastor.

In the form for ordination used by the RCUS we find the following definition of the work of the minister of the Word:

> Dear brother, you are therefore as a servant of Christ to feed the flock of God; to preach the Word in season and out of season; to reprove, to rebuke, to exhort with all patience and humility; to instruct the ignorant, to comfort the afflicted, to strengthen the weak, to seek the lost; to instruct the youth, to continue in prayer and supplication, to administer the holy sacraments, and to maintain good discipline and order in the Church of God.
>
> Be watchful in all things; be a good soldier of Jesus Christ; do the work of an evangelist; make full

proof of your ministry; fight the good fight of faith: then the God of peace will be with you; and the Lord, the righteous Judge, will give you a crown of righteousness at that day. (The Directory of Worship, 1998).

These instructions recognize that the ministry has to do with serving Christ in the capacity of caring for the flock that belongs to Christ. This care comes in several forms. Paul reminds the Ephesian elders of his ministry when he says, "for three years I did not cease night or day to admonish everyone with tears" (Acts 20:31).

I recently heard of someone whose pastor told him that he doesn't do counseling. This individual had just gone through a very difficult time in his life and needed direction and comfort from the word of God and his pastor was unwilling to provide it. In this connection counseling is seen as something that only someone specifically trained in the field of counseling can do. Usually that means humanistic psychology. The message from the Bible, which is a message that speaks to people's situations, is just what this individual needed. Effective counseling is guiding a believer in his need to apply what the word of God says to his particular life situation.

I have also personally known of pastors who are very harsh with the members in counseling situations. To rail at someone for hours because of a particular sinful habit is not only counter-productive, but fails to see the reality of the need which God's people have and how Christ has provided for that need. Yes, sin must be clearly and even forcefully dealt with. At times it is necessary to confront and rebuke, but that rebuke must come out of a genuine concern for a lamb that belongs to God. The Scripture presents such rebuke in the context of genuine care and longsuffering, and accompanied by restoration.

If the only contact that the believer has with the pastor is when he is in trouble and getting chewed out for misbehavior, then he is not being cared for. The pastoral care is much more involved. It involves a formal, passionate, vibrant proclamation of the Word. It involves at times a formal counseling session, but it also involves simply establishing a relationship. A pastor must know his people and must be able to be a real person to them.

Being Guided by the Concept of Comfort

The definition of pastoral ministry then must be based on the following principle: Ministry as presented in the Scripture must grow out of an understanding of who the people being ministered to are and what God intends for them. Once again this is expressed in the Heidelberg Catechism question and answer #1. This introductory question and answer to the creed

> indicates the content of what is to follow and describes Christian comfort as an all-encompassing reality. The secret of Christian comfort is not held in our own hand, but in the faithfulness of the Savior, who has made payment and thus has redeemed us and now takes us into His protection. This interpretation is completely *Christological* in nature and focuses on man's salvation without lapsing into anthropology (Van't Spijker, 2009, p. 97).

Pastoral ministry must not be about rebuking man to better himself. It must be about encouraging the believer to understand and embrace all that Christ has accomplished for him and also to comprehend that Christ's accomplishment is what leads him to take joy in his relationship with his Savior and to respond in thanksgiving. When pastoral ministry approaches the troubled believer from that perspective, the pastor is truly bringing a ministry of comfort to the one who is hurting and troubled about his relationship with God.

This understanding also has implications for the attitude of the pastor. As Christ is concerned to bring comfort to the sinner, so the pastor must have that same concern. While he needs to speak clearly and authoritatively about the truth of God and the consequences of wrong living, he is to do that with great empathy for the condition of the one who is in trouble with God.

When ministry is approached from the perspective that the purpose of ministry is simply to make people feel bad about their sin, then that is all it will accomplish. I am convinced, based on personal observation, that there are pastors who understand their task as being one of simply pointing out just how horrible the sins of their people are. Thus the notion is that the more the reality of sin can be stressed, the more effectively it will cause people to turn away from their sin.

To approach ministry totally from this perspective is to ultimately rely on the ability of the individual to do something about his sin. This will only result in greater frustration and a sense of guilt. While sin needs to be pointed out, and sometimes in very clear and authoritative ways, it is useless if reliance on the finished work of Christ is not presented as the answer to the problem of sin. Thus the concern of the pastor must not be simply to make the sinner feel bad, but to bring him comfort. I again reference the words of the Apostle Paul: "[F]or three years I did not cease night or day to admonish everyone with tears" (Acts 20:31).

Clearly a biblical definition informs the pastor of his ministry as well as his approach to ministry. I point again to the word "pastor" or "shepherd." These words imply a caring ministry which begins with a heart that truly loves God's people because there is an understanding that God loves His people and that ministry is needed for the people to receive comfort in their relationship with God.

Indeed we see how an understanding of both the use of the Church and the goal which God has for His people very much informs our definition of pastoral ministry.

3

AN OVERVIEW OF COVENANT THEOLOGY

The Covenantal Perspective

Covenant theology begins with the simple notion that God from eternity has one plan of salvation, and that this one plan of salvation is progressively revealed by means of God's dealing with His people throughout Scripture. God's purpose in this one plan of salvation is to separate unto Himself a people who are the one church of God. It is this people, having been separated unto Himself, with whom God makes a covenant. The principle involved in covenant making is that God comes to lost sinners and obligates Himself to provide salvation. By means of this covenantal relationship the people of God are promised the hope of eternal life because it is God who has claimed them and who keeps them. The emphasis is upon the fact that God takes an oath and swears by His name to be God to His people. This means that He will take care of them and provide for their every need, including salvation. In the following passage we see a demonstration of this relationship.

> But the LORD's portion is his people, Jacob his allotted heritage. He found him in a desert land, and in the howling waste of the wilderness; he encircled him, he cared for him, he kept him as the apple of his eye. Like an eagle that stirs up its nest, that flutters over its young, spreading out its wings, catching them, bearing them on its pinions, the LORD alone guided him, no foreign god was with him. He made him ride on the high places of the land, and he ate the

produce of the field, and he suckled him with honey out of the rock, and oil out of the flinty rock.

Curds from the herd, and milk from the flock, with fat of lambs, rams of Bashan and goats, with the very finest of the wheat--and you drank foaming wine made from the blood of the grape (Deut. 32:9-14).

In the New Testament the Apostle Paul describes the privilege of receiving covenant blessings as he speaks of the oneness of the people of God:

And he came and preached peace to you who were far off and peace to those who were near. For through him we both have access in one Spirit to the Father. So then you are no longer strangers and aliens, but you are fellow citizens with the saints and members of the household of God, built on the foundation of the apostles and prophets, Christ Jesus himself being the cornerstone, in whom the whole structure, being joined together, grows into a holy temple in the Lord. In him you also are being built together into a dwelling place for God by the Spirit (Eph. 2:17-22).

This relationship is dependent upon what God has done and thus the claim He makes on His people. It also provides a certain assurance for the believer because the relationship is based on God.

The Covenant Concept Initiated in the Garden

When God created Adam and Eve, He created them in His image, He put them in the garden of Eden and He required that they live in obedience before Him. From the creation account (Gen. 1-2) we learn several important things about the created relationship between God and man. Man is created a unique creature, a unique task is given to him to carry out for God, and He is to live in harmony with God's direction. Even though the particular terminology is not used in the creation account, reformed scholars consider this a covenant relationship (Robertson, 1980, p. 25). It is a covenant relationship in that God has established the conditions by which man is to live before God and the stipulations include clear blessings or curses based on this relationship.

The clear implication of this covenant relationship is that God has created man in such a way that what is normative for man is to be in a life giving, loving relationship with God his creator. Thus there is a connection between understanding this covenantal relationship and considering the pastoral ministry. To help understand the implications for ministry it will be helpful to see the development of God's covenant-making in Scripture. Therefore, before I proceed with the various aspects of ministry I will give a brief presentation of the covenant of grace as we see it unfolded in Scripture.

When Adam disobeyed, the special relationship with God was broken. The God of love, demonstrating His grace, however, provided for that relationship to be restored. By means of the immediate promise which God made in Genesis 3:15, life is continued. God works toward the fulfilling of this promise by means of repeated covenant-making which points to full restoration in Christ. Following the life, death, resurrection, and ascension of Christ the fullness of that covenant relationship is realized. The church in the New Testament is established based on this reality.

Christianity is about being right with God through trust in the work of Christ, and thus being assured of eternal life. The true believer is assured in God's word that he is right with God and will not face the wrath of God which burns against sin. This is a great gift from God through Jesus Christ. However, there is a great deal more to having salvation. I believe American Christianity has reduced faith in Christ to a very small aspect of life and is thus missing out on the richness of being the people of God. This is obviously my opinion based on my understanding of the emphases that are common among Christians in general. The exaggerated emphasis upon a personal faith and "decisionism" (Matto, 2013) has, in my opinion, led to this narrow understanding of salvation.

Being right with God involves having a relationship with God. We must not think that this relationship first begins when the believer goes to heaven. Clearly, God calls His people unto Himself and establishes them as His own. This relationship is for the purpose of a restored fellowship with God (I Pet. 2:9).

Belonging to God is noted in Scripture as being in covenant with God. The covenantal relationship is very important in understanding how we now live in fellowship with God. As indicated, the purpose of this study is to examine how ministry is to function in a pastoral way. Having a relationship with God and living in His presence is pastoral by nature. To seriously deal with the pastoral nature of the ministry we must begin with the basic concept of being in covenant with God.

Heidelberg catechism Question #1, which is referred to in chapter 1, raises the question of comfort: "What is your only comfort in life and in death?" The answer is based on what God does for the believer. What God has done is establish a covenant relationship. This is laid out for us in Scripture in a progressive way; we see it fully in the New Testament.

God made a covenant with Noah following the flood, when He promised He would never again destroy the earth by means of a flood. Part of this agreement was that God would provide for a means to keep sin in check. What we want to see here is the reason for this is not God just felt bad about the flood and did not want to send another one. He established the possibility of having a people, called out of this world, that could still live in this world and enjoy life in His presence. Thus by means of the covenant with Noah God has established a context in which sin will not run rampant in an absolute way. God's people will not again be swallowed up as they were in Genesis 6-7, and God will establish a special relationship with those whom He seeks to make a covenant with.

The Covenant Continued and Expanded Upon

Even though there were individuals who knew God prior to Abraham, it is with Abraham that God begins to separate a people unto Himself and claim them in a special relationship. The emphasis which has been placed upon the account concerning Abraham is that God calls His own and separates them from the world. God called Abraham out of Ur, a great pagan city (Gen. 12). The principle that God provides all that is needed for man to be in covenant is also established with Abraham. God provides the surety of the covenant. This is demonstrated by the covenant making we see in Genesis 15, where God provides the seed of the covenant through the miraculous birth of Isaac, Abraham's son. This is reemphasized when God commands Abraham to sacrifice his son but then provides a lamb for the sacrifice instead.

As the people of God are initially established in Abraham, we begin to see the concept of God claiming a people for Himself. God has called them, God has provided the means of salvation, and God has claimed them with the sign of the covenant. Abraham was required to circumcise all the males in his household (Gen. 17). This is to identify the separateness of His people and the fact that God does cleanse from sin. The fact that circumcision is a sign in which blood is shed is important here. It points forward to the shedding of blood by Christ.

In Exodus 2:24, when the descendants of Abraham find themselves in Egypt under the cruel conditions of slavery, God remembers the covenant He had made. The entire account of the exodus from Egypt demonstrates the reality of sin, its absolute control and its destructive nature. The children of Israel cannot live and survive under slavery. They are totally dependent upon God to bring relief. In the process of being rescued from slavery, the notion of a sacrifice to cover for sin is emphasized.

In saving His people, God brings the plagues on Egypt and demonstrates the fact that He destroys sin. With the tenth plague we see the need for a sacrifice. Blood is shed so that a remedy is provided for God's people to escape the angel of death. The reality is that the Israelites and the Egyptians are in the same situation; they both are under the threat of the angel of death, which is simply the rightfully deserved punishment for sin. The children of Israel escape only because of what God does for them. He provides a sacrifice, and those who have the covering of blood from this sacrifice escape the punishment from the angel of death. All of this is based on what God provides.

The progression of God establishing His people now moves to the point of God's people becoming a nation as they invade the land of promise, destroy the Canaanites, and establish the nation of Israel. Even though the people continuously fail to be all that God has called them to be, God does provide for the nation of Israel to become a powerful and important nation. The height of this development is under King David. David fought the enemies of God, expanded the border of Israel and achieved a certain peace with Israel's neighbors. Thus David epitomizes the notion of a people who are separate; a people who are ruled and protected by God. King David represents the rule of God over His people.

The Scriptures here again speak of a covenant relationship as God makes a promise with David in II Samuel 7 that his house, meaning his dynasty, would be king forever. This is fulfilled when Jesus is born the son of David (Luke 1:32), and is seated at the right side of God upon His ascension into heaven (Acts 2:34).

In all of this we have the concept of God calling His people, God providing a covering for the sin of His people, and God providing for His people to be led and protected. All of these things point forward to the reality of God's relationship with His people as it comes to its fullness in the New Testament.

In the Old Testament the actual relationship is an outward relationship, with the land, the temple, and the sacrificial system being at the heart of that outward covenant relationship with God. This eventually fails with the destruction of Israel and the people being taken into captivity. But based on this outward covenant relationship, God promises a new covenant which will have an inward reality (Jer. 31:31-34). The same God, calling a people unto Himself on the same covenantal relationship, promises that the law of God will no longer be simply written on stone, but on the hearts of God's people.

The Covenant Concept Continued in the New Testament

The Old Testament covenant making and the established relationship between God and His people provide the background of the Church being established in the book of Acts. In reality, God's people are ultimately identified as such not by means of a nation or a race of people, but by belonging to Him in Spirit and truth. It is the promises of the covenant which Peter gives as the basis for God's people and their children to be baptized (Acts 2:38-39). Those for whom Jesus is the lamb and who are covered by the blood of Jesus--thus escaping the eternal punishment for sin--truly belong to God through Jesus Christ. This is what Jesus speaks of when He says, "My sheep hear my voice, and I know them, and they follow me" (John 10:27).

The writer to the Hebrews picks up on the covenant concept in pointing out that now the law of God is not written on tablets of stone but on our hearts. The fact that God claims His people in a covenant relationship is not set aside but in fact is enhanced with the Holy Spirit. The apostle Peter uses covenantal language in describing the Church in the following manner:

> But you are a chosen generation, a royal priesthood, a holy nation, His own special people that you may proclaim the praises of Him who called you out of darkness into His marvelous light; who once were not a people but are now the people of God, who had not obtained mercy but now have obtained mercy (I Peter 2:9-10).

The Implications of the Covenantal Concept

Pastoral ministry must be seen as a ministry to God's people whom God has claimed as His own by means of the covenant. The answer to Heidelberg catechism Q&A #1 is "that I belong to my faithful Savior, Jesus Christ" (The Three Forms, p. 19, 2001). It is that relationship of ownership, of God's claim for His people whom He has purchased and established as uniquely His, to which pastors are called to be shepherds in order to take care of God's flock.

In Acts 20, Paul exhorts the elders concerning their task of being shepherds to the people of God. I believe that the reference to elders here is more in line with the office of pastor today. But the point is that the exhortation to take care of the flock is based on the fact that the flock belongs to God. They have been purchased by Christ with His blood. They are God's precious possession. He gives them to the elders to care for, as a steward would for a master: "Pay careful attention to yourselves and to all the flock, in which the Holy Spirit has made you overseers, to care for the church of God, which he obtained with his own blood" (Acts 20:28).

The message from God captured in the Heidelberg Catechism Q&A #1 is that true comfort is from God. That is at the heart of what God's grace is all about. God made man with everything being just fine, man destroyed himself, man brought on the misery, and man did all to the point that he is without hope in his own situation. It is at this point that God comes to man, while man is at enmity with God, and provides new life. God's message comes from God to man so that man who has rebelled and hates God might have life. That is the gospel.

The foundation of this message of comfort is based in the reality of belonging to God, "that I belong to my faithful Savior" (The Three Forms, p. 19, 2001). Without comfort there can only be misery which is the result of Satan destroying the relationship in order to get man away from God. God does not just come and say "it's okay, you can come back." No, God sovereignly reaches out to His people and says, "You belong to me, I am your God and you shall be my people."

This relationship of belonging to God and having comfort is possible because "the blood of Jesus Christ cleanses us from all sin" (I John 1:7). When Christ went to the cross he took on and paid for our sinful nature and for every sin that the believer has or ever will commit and thus bore the full weight of God's wrath against sin. That means that the basis for our relationship with God has absolutely nothing to do with what we have done. It is based on what God has done for us through Christ, and the message of comfort is to tell us about that fact.

Reliance upon God and not upon Man

This gives the believer a great sense of certainty with regard to life before God. True comfort is not based on circumstances in life, but on the love of Christ upon which we can count (Rom. 8:35). We can be assured that the love of Christ can and will keep us. The believer can know that his comfort, which is based on God and not on man, covers all that life is: he belongs to God, not to himself.

It is also important to notice that as the writers of the Heidelberg Catechism present this comfort, it is not something that is available based on certain conditions being met. It does not say that this is the good news if you are a good person, or if you do certain things, or if you decide to take it. Even more to the point, it does not say that you can have comfort because you can consider the strength of your faith, or because you have had some special experience after a life of struggle. Rather it speaks of a comfort which is yours based on the fact that you belong to your faithful Savior Jesus Christ. It is God simply telling us that He has determined to make us His own. It is the work of God, accomplished by God, signed, sealed and delivered.

That does not mean that the people of God may do with their life as they desire, that they can ignore the law of God, come to church only when they feel like it and be ignorant of what God says in His word. The one to whom God has brought this comfort is indeed a child of God. He loves God, he seeks to know what this message of comfort is all about and he truly delights in serving Jesus with all his life.

This brings us right back to covenantal ministry. The context of this ministry is the people who belong to God, who are His precious possession. They need a shepherd to care for them. It is through this shepherd that Christ cares for them.

4

COVENANTAL WORSHIP

The underlying concept which we see in the covenant God has established between Himself and man, who is the image bearer of God, is one of an ongoing relationship. Understanding how this relationship functions is very important in meeting the needs that God's people have for nourishment. We begin with the covenant community coming before God in worship. While worship was always very important as I grew up in a small, rural church, I am not sure that the reason for worshiping God and the principles involved were always that clear. Certainly it was understood that God requires worship, but what is God's purpose in this requirement?

It is no secret that there is much discussion today about worship and the approach people take toward it. Many have strong opinions about what they like or do not like about different approaches toward worship. Some have even referred to the current debate concerning worship as the "worship wars" (Hart & Muether, 2002, p. 12). I am convinced that often such discussions center on what individuals like or do not like from a very personal perspective. Many decide what church to attend based on which worship service seems to meet their personal tastes the best. However, biblical worship ought never to be driven by personal tastes, but rather by the principles derived from Scripture. There is a real need for the worshiping community to have a more biblically based set of principles by which worship is understood and practiced.

Worship as a Pattern for Life

God put man in the Garden of Eden to live before Him in this creation and to enjoy life in His presence. This was broken by sin and is restored in Christ. But the important thing is to understand that all of life is before God and in service to God. Yet there is a very important distinction between worshipping and living before God. We use the word worship to describe that activity by which we meet with God to praise Him and be fed by His Word. We also understand that for the rest of our life we are to live before God and to meet His purpose for us; we call this service.

These two aspects of life are very closely related and yet very distinct from each other. It is important that we do not confuse them. The principle for this pattern of life is established in the creation and spelled out in the fourth commandment with the direction to work and rest. Work is serving God in His creation; rest is meeting with Him face to face for the sustenance of life itself.

Worship is Covenantal in Nature

To understand that the basic nature of man as created by God is to be in fellowship with God, we also need to understand what effect sin had on this nature. When Adam sinned the relationship was cut off. The prohibition against sin was clearly stated in that man would die when he ate of the fruit of the tree of the knowledge of good and evil. The biblical account demonstrates the break in that when God came to man following the fall, Adam and Eve hid from God. They were ashamed. It is God who comes to them and by grace reestablishes the relationship. The answer to man's failure in the test of obedience, was that God by grace provided restoration of that fellowship through the promised seed (Gen. 3:15). Even though man was put out of the garden to remind him of his need for grace, the avenue for fellowship with God was provided.

The promise of a seed by which the head of the serpent will be crushed is ultimately fulfilled in Christ. Christ is spoken of in Romans 5 as the second Adam because he accomplished with his life and sacrifice what the first Adam could not. Following the fall into sin the covenant relationship continued based on grace. As a result of the covenant, fellowship with God is now once again basic to the relationship between God and man. As we consider worship and the principles underlying worship we must begin with the basic fact that worship is covenantal in nature. It is the covenant community, with God promising to be God to a special people who respond to him in faith, which then calls upon Him in worship. It has been suggested that worship is a "covenant renewal ceremony":

> It is in this context that we talk about the "covenant renewal ceremony." Whenever we gather for public worship, it is because we have been summoned. That is what "church" means: *ekklesia*, "called out." It is not a voluntary society of those whose chief concern is to share, to build community, to enjoy fellowship, to have moral instruction for their children, and so forth. Rather, it is a society of those who have been chosen, redeemed, called, justified, and are being sanctified until one day they will finally be glorified in heaven. We gather each Lord's Day not merely out of habit, social custom, or felt needs but because God has chosen this weekly festival as a foretaste of the everlasting Sabbath day that will be enjoyed fully at the marriage supper of the Lamb. God has called us out of the world and into his marvelous light: That is why we gather (Horton, 2002, p. 24).

The emphasis in covenant making is the notion that God has called a people, He has made them special, and He has set them apart as a community which calls upon Him to praise His name. Specifically, they are set apart through the work of Christ; the mediator of the covenant. In his book on worship Hughes Oliphant Old (2002), states it this way:

Christian worship is in the name of Christ because worship is a function of the body of Christ and as Christians we are all one body. All of our worship must be in him! What an important New Testament concept this is that the church is the body of Christ, and how vividly the first Christians understood that they were all together one body, the body of Christ. They understood their worship to be part of the worship that the ascended Christ performed in the heavenly sanctuary to the glory of the Father (Heb. 7:23-25; 9:25; 10:19-22; 13:15) (p. 4).

When we speak of worship as being by the body of Christ we are speaking of the covenant community.

To speak of worship as being covenantal is then also to say that worship is "otherworldly" (Hart & Muether, 2002, p. 25). That is, worship is not to be guided by the principles which are attractive to the world. The antithesis which exists between the church and the world is not to be ignored when the Church worships.

J. Gresham Machen, who battled worldliness in the church through his whole life, had little trouble defending the idea that the church should be separate from the world. In "The Separateness of the Church," a sermon he preached at Princeton Seminary in 1925 on Matthew 5:13 ("You are the salt of the earth...."), Machen declared that these words of Christ "established at the very beginning the distinctness and separateness of the Church." If the distinction between the church and the world was ever lost, Machen warned, "the power of the Church is gone. The Church then becomes like salt that has lost its savor, and is fit only to be cast out and to be trodden under foot of men" (Hart & Muether, 2002, p. 25).

An additional implication of worship being covenantal is that it properly connects worship with the rest of life. It is crucial to maintain the distinction between corporate worship and the service (worship) that the believer offers to God in all of life (Rom. 12:1). It is equally crucial to understand that every aspect of life is to be lived in service to God. When the covenant community meets with God to praise Him and to hear His message it is being prepared to work for God. As the people of God live their lives in the world they seek to serve God in all that they are involved in.

> You can worship God in your job at an office or factory, by serving on a community committee, by planting a garden or making a crewel picture. This does not negate the importance of corporate worship on the Lord's day but rather it prepares you for corporate praise. The Sunday assembly in turn should send you forth eager to glorify God in the situations that occur during the ensuing week. True worship cannot be isolated from all we are in life nor can true living be isolated from worship (Engle, 1978, p. 94).

Examining the Pictures of Worship in the Bible

The Scriptures have a great deal to say about worship. There are four basic pictures given in Scripture that I find establish the basic principles for worship. The fundamental principle for worship is that which is established in the fourth commandment. God sets forth here the purpose for man: it is to serve God with a particular pattern of life. The pattern is six days of work and one of rest; six days of serving God in His creation and one of intimate fellowship with God. The rest speaks of the spiritual need which man has, but that spiritual aspect is not divorced from serving God in all of life. All of life then, both work and rest, is the fulfillment of who man is: an image bearer of God created to live in the life sustained for him by God. Keeping in mind this basic principle, the pictures in Scripture which we will now examine establish how the principle of work and rest becomes a reality for God's people.

The Establishment of Public Worship

We begin with the second part of Genesis 4:26: "At that time people began to call upon the name of the Lord." In Genesis 4-5 there is a brief history of two kinds of people. These chapters present the line of Seth, which is the people of God, and the line of Cain, which is the ungodly line. Established here are the basic characteristics of their life.

Genesis 5:1 states that this is the genealogy of Adam, a family history if you will. This is not a complete history. It is not even really a history, the reference is more in the sense of "this is their story, this is who they are." This is a presentation of the character of the people of God. In the previous chapter is the life, or the characteristic of the ungodly. We read of Cain naming a city after his son (Gen. 4:17). We also read of Lamech, who says to his wives that if anyone gets in his way he will kill him (Genesis 4:23). The characteristic of the life of the ungodly is that life is about the individual, about man. It is an attempt to get away from being dependent upon God. It is this approach to life which ultimately leads to the need for God to destroy the earth with the flood in Genesis 6-8.

To understand the character of the life of the godly we need to go back to the beginning of chapter four when Eve names her first son following the promise of God concerning the continuing of life. In verse one Eve names her son Cain and states, "I have gotten a man with the help of the Lord." The name literally means that Adam and Eve received a human. This is the first record of a birth, which points to the continuation of life. So now they are fully aware that they should be dead, yet here is a son. It is the sign of ongoing life. The promise given by God is that of the seed. This is a seed. Eve gives credit to the Lord. By means of this name she acknowledges, perhaps very primitively, but a genuine faith in the promise.

Obviously, Cain, who murdered his brother, did not turn out to be the seed in terms of the continuation of the covenant promise. When they have a third son we see again that in naming him Seth, Eve expresses her faith in that the name means "the substitute." Eve's faith is passed on to the next generation when Seth has a son and names him Enosh which means "the frail one, the dependent one," (Keil & Delitzsch, 1973, p. 119). Notice the sharp contrast between Cain naming a city after his son, and Seth giving his son a name which indicates being dependent upon God.

All of this is to understand first of all that the godly are a people who believe in God. They express their faith in the promise of God. This leads to this statement at the end of Genesis 4 "At that time people began to call upon the name of the Lord" (Gen. 4:26b). There is an emphasis upon the first word in the sentence which in the original is translated by the ESV "at that time." As we then look at the statement in Genesis 4:26b, it indicates that a people who are dependent upon God are a people with a basic principle of life. This principle, established by means of the story of the godly, is that they are a people who are characterized by faith. As people of faith they are then also a people who call upon God. This is the beginning of public worship. The idea of worship--calling upon God as being dependent upon the Creator-- is engrained in man in that he is created in the image of God.

So as life begins on earth--life by sinful, fallen men--there are those who trust in themselves and there are those who trust in God. Those who trust in God are a people who call upon Him in worship. The first picture we have of public worship in the Scriptures is that it is what people of faith do. It is a fundamental character of the godly. Worship is not an option, it is not something men do because it is appealing, or any other outward attraction. Rather, it reflects the basic character of man who is right with God.

God Meets with His People in Worship

An ongoing difficulty in the Old Testament concerning God meeting with His people was the fact that sin was not yet paid for by Christ. God provided an outward covering in Genesis 3:21 which pointed to the sacrifice of Christ. Yet throughout the Old Testament man could not come directly into the presence of God and live. Sin stood between them. The holy God cannot have sin or sinful man in His presence, yet as the covenant God His desire is to meet with His people and they are dependent upon Him. After the renewing of the covenant in Exodus 19, God directed the people to meet with Him at Mount Sinai, but they were warned not to touch the mountain. The entire time of meeting with God was a frightful, bad experience for the people. As a result they asked that Moses meet with God from then on (Exodus 20:18-19).

This leaves a dilemma: how can God be with His people as they are in the wilderness and yet not consume them? In Numbers chapter two we are given a description of the camp for life in the wilderness as directed by God. A major aspect of this is the tabernacle. The tabernacle provided that God could be present by means of the inner sanctuary or "Holy of Holies." God's most complete presence was in the Holy of Holies. Thus He was in the midst of His people, yet they did not have direct contact with Him. The only contact with God that they had was through the service of the priesthood. The tabernacle--the portable place of worship-- provided for God's people to have access to God and be directed by Him in life.

Numbers chapter two shows how the camp was set up with the tabernacle in its midst. The people camped in twelve tribes around the tabernacle. In between the tabernacle and the people were the Levites who provided for the service of the tabernacle. When they camped or when they marched God was always in their midst by means of the tabernacle. It is particularly important to note the description of this arrangement as it is described in verses two and twenty-two. Each tribe had its own standard. The standard identified who the people were according to the tribe and it marked where they camped and traveled. But it also marked the connection the tribe had with God: "The people of Israel shall camp each by his own standard, with the banners of their fathers' houses. They shall camp facing the tent of meeting on every side" (Num. 2:22).

It is a bit difficult to get the full sense of this verse, but it does indicate that by means of the standard, there is a line of sight by which the people of each tribe are connected to the tabernacle, thus with God. We also read this concerning their travel: "Then the tent of meeting shall set out, with the camp of the Levites in the midst of the camps; as they camp, so shall they set out, each in position, standard by standard" (Num. 2:17). Once again close contact between God and His people is maintained by means of the tribes and their standards.

This entire picture is that of life for the people of God in a very concentrated form as they live and travel in the wilderness. The principle is that life is before God. Notice that the tabernacle was not set up for worship and then taken down again. Neither was the tabernacle set up off to the side so that those who wanted to could go there to worship when they wanted to. Rather, it was in the center of the camp and it was always there. Now, there was a particular means of formal worship, but God was still central in all aspects of their life. They worshiped God, they traveled with God, and they camped with God. In every way and with every thought God was central to them.

The principle which is so fundamental here is that worship and fellowship with God do not only apply to one small part of life. It is central to life. Life is service before and unto God. This life is both worship in the formal sense and service (worship) in the form of living before God and following Him by means of His direction. The Old Testament people did not have the complete revelation of God as we do today. They needed specific direction from God. The revelation from God was a guide for life. Today we have the full revelation for life from God in the Scriptures, and the principle is that we still need to have God central in everything that we do. God's covenant people live and worship with their eyes upon God.

Direct Access to God is Provided by Christ

What we have seen in the Old Testament picture is that God, by means of the tabernacle and the priesthood, provided a way by which He could meet with His people both in formal worship and as they lived in His presence. Restoration with God is accomplished through the Messiah, our Savior Jesus Christ. While meeting with God is typified through the tabernacle and priesthood it is made real by Christ in the new covenant. The author of the book of Hebrews says this concerning our access into the presence of God:

> Therefore, brothers, since we have confidence to enter the holy places by the blood of Jesus, by the new and living way that he opened for us through the curtain, that is, through his flesh, and since we have a great priest over the house of God, let us draw near with a true heart in full assurance of faith, with our hearts sprinkled clean from an evil conscience and our bodies washed with pure water (Heb. 10:19-22).

Jesus Himself is now the curtain through which we come into the presence of God, which is implied in the reference to "entering the holy places." The blood which is sprinkled is that of Jesus. This statement is in the context of an exhortation by the author for the public gathering of God's people in worship. The implication is that when Christ offered Himself for our sins on the cross and the veil of the temple was torn, access to meet with God face to face was opened to all believers. We no longer need priests to represent us before God.

This picture presents a very important principle concerning New Testament worship: When God's people gather corporately for public worship and they do so in the name of Christ, they are by faith coming into the Holy of Holies in the temple of the living God, the new Jerusalem (Heb. 12:22ff). To meet with God is truly an experience through which God's people are fed, and by which their spiritual needs are met. This is the ultimate pastoral provision for God's people.

Worship Takes Place in the City of the Living God

The author of Hebrews gives a most complete picture of New Testament worship in chapter 12. He begins by comparing the notion of coming to God as it was experienced at Mount Sinai and at Mount Zion. At Mount Sinai it was a horrible experience because the blood of Christ had not yet covered for sin (Exod. 19).

In contrast, now worship is described as follows: "But you have come to Mount Zion and to the city of the living God, the heavenly Jerusalem" (Heb. 12:22). By faith God's people in worship meet with God in the new temple built without hands. That is, we come directly into the presence of God, in the most intimate of fellowship with Him. This is further described as coming before the angels, meeting with all the saints who have gone before us, to Jesus who is the mediator of the new covenant, and to God who is the judge of all. Coming to God--the judge of all--based on the sprinkled blood of Christ, indicates that all those coming before God have been judged righteous.

We have just briefly touched on four pictures given in the Scriptures concerning worship. However, what is abundantly clear is that worship is meeting with God.

> What is it that makes the assembly of the church unique? Why is it different from other types of meeting? The church is different because it is an assembly of God's people *in his very presence*. The assembling of the church is a meeting with God as well as with fellow believers. The assembly is an extraordinary, supernatural event. This is implicit in the very term *church* (Engle, 1978, p. 15).

Based on the redemption we have in Christ our whole life is restored to God. Keep in mind that God created a pattern for life; that is living before Him and coming to Him in worship.

If worship is meeting with God, then there must be communication with God. God speaks to His people and His people respond. How does He speak? The biblical understanding of worship, in the context of meeting with God, is that in reality Jesus Himself speaks by means of ordained ministers preaching from the Scriptures. This is implied by the Apostle Paul when he states this series of redundant questions: "How then will they call on him in whom they have not believed? And how are they to believe in him (of) whom they have never heard? And how are they to hear without someone preaching?" (Rom. 10:14).

I placed parenthesis around the word "of" in the second question because the best translation does not include this word. The implication is that when ministers who are faithful to the revealed Word are preaching during corporate worship they are not telling the congregation something "of" Jesus. Rather, in that context it is Jesus Himself who is speaking to His people (Hendriksen, 1981, p. 348, note 295).

This simply underscores again the greatness and intimacy of worship. Truly participating in worship is the most fundamental means by which God's people are provided for spiritually. From a Reformed perspective the preaching of the Word has always been seen as central to the work of the ministry. I would certainly maintain that concept. But I would add that it is also important to approach this important aspect of ministry with the understanding that the purpose is to meet the pastoral needs of the sheep. Those needs include both instruction and encouragement.

Worship as a Celebration of the Resurrection of Christ

Heidelberg Catechism Q&A #21 asks, "What is true faith?" The answer begins with stating that it is "not only a sure knowledge whereby I hold for truth all that God has revealed to us in His Word, but also a hearty trust, which the Holy Spirit works in me by the Gospel" (The Three Forms, 2000, p. 7). In stating that faith includes having a hearty trust the Catechism establishes that there is a heartfelt emotional aspect to Christianity. In the same way that the "sure knowledge" of faith must be addressed by ongoing teaching and preaching of the content of the word of God, the "hearty trust" aspect of faith must be addressed. It is here where the pastoral aspect of ministry specifically comes into play.

This pastoral aspect involves a number of things which will be addressed in a later chapter, but it also must be grounded in formal worship. A Reformed understanding of worship sees the preaching of the Word as central, and that preaching is to be a serious exposition of the biblical text. This is exactly how preaching ought to be viewed. The problem arises when a focus on the centrality of preaching makes the remainder of worship unimportant. If we understand that worship is meeting with God, then all that we do in worship ought to reflect the awesome privilege of meeting with God. All of worship ought to receive as much attention in terms of being well planned and put together as the preparation for the preaching of the Word does. My own experience has been that all too often, very little attention is given to the non-preaching aspects of worship. In most situations in the RCUS, where ministers are expected to do everything, it is very difficult to find the time needed for careful planning of the various aspects of worship.

There are two very important elements in worship which can appear to be contradictory but ought not to be. We approach God with a deep sense of awe and reverence, and even sober mindedness. But at the same time, we understand that in meeting with God there is a certain anticipation and excitement. It is properly an emotional experience. A cursory reading of the Psalms indicates there is a considerable emotional aspect to worship.

In my experience as a pastor I have often commented that it would be good for members of the congregation to have the perspective of the preacher as he looks into the faces of God's people during worship. All too often the faces look as though they were at a funeral. The Psalmist says, "I was glad when they said to me, 'Let us go to the house of the Lord!'" (Ps. 122:1). I would suggest this is an expression of awe and joy properly put together as a stance for worship.

In the early chapters of Acts, when the followers of Christ first began to worship following His ascension, they met on the first day of the week because they celebrated the resurrection of Christ that had taken place on the first day of the week. I have often stated that in reality, every Lord's Day is Easter, meaning that it is a celebration of the resurrection of Christ.

> The ancient church viewed the Sunday mainly, we may say, one-sidedly and exclusively, from its Christian aspect as a new institution, and not in any way as a continuation of the Jewish Sabbath. It observed it as the day of the commemoration of the resurrection or of the new spiritual creation, and hence a day of sacred joy and thanksgiving, standing in bold contrast to the days of humiliation and fasting, as the Easter festival contrasts with Good Friday (Schaff, 1910, p. 379).

One of the basic elements of early Christian life and worship was Christian fellowship (Acts 2:42). This reflected an emphasis on the mutual joy of believers celebrating with each other. In the book of Revelation we find a picture of the future consummated worship in heaven where worship vibrates with songs of praise (Engle, 1978, p. 3-4).

By the fourth century there had been a shift in emphasis from a celebration of the resurrection of Christ to a remembrance of the death of Christ, as the sacrament of the Lord's Supper came to be seen as a re-sacrifice of Christ.

> According to this doctrine the Eucharist is an unbloody repetition of the atoning sacrifice of Christ by the priesthood for the salvation of the living and the dead; so that the body of Christ is truly and literally offered every day and every hour and upon innumerable altars at the same time (Schaff, 1910, p. 504).

This shift which came to its fullness during the Middle Ages had significant influence on how all of worship was approached. Worship now appeared to be more in tune with the idea of a funeral rather than a wedding feast.

> ...yet that old sacrificial service, which was interwoven with the whole popular life of the Jewish and Graeco-Roman world, exerted a controlling influence on the Roman Catholic service of the Eucharist, especially after nominal conversion of the

whole Roman heathendom, and obscured the original simplicity and purity of that service almost beyond recognition (Schaff, 1910, p. 505).

The reformers rejected and condemned the notion of the re-sacrifice of Christ in the sacrament, as evidenced by Heidelberg Catechism Q&A #80:

> What difference is there between the Lord's Supper and the Pope's Mass?
>
> The Lord's Supper testifies to us that we have full forgiveness of all our sins by the one sacrifice of Jesus Christ, which He Himself once accomplished on the cross; and that by the Holy Spirit we are engrafted into Christ, who, with His true body, is now in heaven at the right hand of the Father, and is there to be worshiped. But the Mass teaches that the living and the dead do not have forgiveness of sins through the sufferings of Christ, unless Christ is still daily offered for them by the priests, and that Christ is bodily under the form of bread and wine, and is therefore to be worshiped in them. And thus the Mass at bottom is nothing else than a denial of the one sacrifice and suffering of Jesus Christ, and an accursed idolatry (The Three Forms, 2000).

The liturgy of the reformers maintained a sense of coming before God with confession of sins and a pardon (Engle, 1978, p. 116). With the Puritans there developed such a strong emphasis on the sermon and the call to struggle with sin that the remaining aspects of worship perhaps faded somewhat into the background (Engle, 1978, p. 114).

In my childhood there was such an emphasis upon reverence and awe when one entered into church that it would have been unthinkable to even smile and have a sense of joy and excitement in worship. I believe that conservative Reformed worship has to some extent lost the celebratory aspect of worship. The reformer Zwingli apparently sought to address the attitude in worship "with catchy illustrations and humor such that people were actually known to laugh in the cathedral in Zurich, Switzerland. Ulrich Zwingli was the preacher who dared to break the somberness of medieval worship" (Engle, 1978, p. 113).

In what is often referred to as contemporary worship, there is concerted effort to make worship exciting and appealing. This has developed into what I call a "pep rally" type of celebration. Such a celebration is manufactured and has the potential to artificially create a sense of excitement. I am not promoting this type of celebration.

What I am promoting, however, is a real sense of the joy that should be in the heart of the believer when he enters into the presence of God in worship and should be, in fact, evident on his face. It is simply an emphasis upon the grace of God and the reality of that grace in the life of the believer. This approach to worship begins with the individual. Yet, the manner in which worship is planned and put together is important in promoting such an approach. We should not simply assume that the believer is aware of how to approach worship based on the manner in which the church has always done it. There is a need to lead the congregation to a healthy concept of worship by teaching and by example. This begins with preparation for worship.

To assist the reader I have included an order of worship as Appendix A. This is the order of worship which I am currently using. There are some variations from week to week which is also indicated. Notice that there is a definite distinction between preparation for worship, worshiping in the presence of God, and then leaving with God's blessing. This reflects the basic requirements of worship which are spelled out in *The Directory of Worship for the RCUS*.

True meaningful worship comes from the heart. We do not seek man-made emotionalism in worship; true worship is not merely going through the motions. There is a connection between spending time with God personally or as a family by communing with God in the Word and prayer and being prepared to have meaningful worship in the corporate context.

One cannot isolate private and public worship into separate compartments. As one's private worship develops, one's appreciation for public worship grows, and vice versa. A person who has had a week of vital communion with God will be best prepared to enter into the fullness of corporate praise. Likewise, assembly on the Lord's day can stimulate enriched private devotion during the ensuing week. Each feeds the other (Engle, 1978, p. 125).

Indeed, there is a connection between worship and work or life apart from formal worship, as spoken of earlier in this chapter. In ministering to God's people and being the shepherd to whom the sheep of Christ (Acts 20:28) have been entrusted for feeding, the pastor needs to be very aware of how he is preparing the members for living before God in all of life. This not only involves encouraging members to have a consistent devotional life, but also involves teaching how to apply biblical principles in every part of their life. As the Israelites viewed the centrality of God in worship and in life, as seen in Numbers chapter 2, so faithful covenantal pastoring involves keeping God before God's people as they go about their lives Monday through Saturday.

5

FEEDING THROUGH THE WORD

Biblical ministry is about bringing together and caring for the people of God. The Scripture certainly teaches that the covenantal care of the people of God is to be accomplished by preaching. The very concept of covenantal care is to provide the spiritual feeding which is basic to the well being of God's people. It would not at all be an overstatement to say that preaching is central to pastoral ministry. This was certainly the emphasis of the reformers. For the Apostle Paul, preaching is not just something which he recommends because it is popular and it is a way to speak of the truths of God. He clearly teaches that preaching is the means ordained by God for His people to hear His word and it is the means by which God works effectively in the hearts of His people:

> For since, in the wisdom of God, the world through wisdom did not know God, it pleased God through the foolishness of the message preached to save those who believe. For Jews request a sign, and Greeks seek after wisdom; but we preach Christ crucified, to the Jews a stumbling block and to the Greeks foolishness, but to those who are called, both Jews and Greeks, Christ the power of God and the wisdom of God (I Cor. 1:21-24).

It is important to understand that the word of God teaches not only that preaching is commanded for the Church, but also it is the tool which God will use to both call His people and to provide for their nourishment. There is a constant temptation to be impatient with this God-ordained means because man does not always see the results that he desires. Man's fertile mind then seeks to find other ways that seem to be popular and in a sense appear to be working. It is important for the Church to maintain the centrality of preaching. It is equally important for the Church to provide preaching that is truly biblical and nourishing.

Preaching as the Word of God

What is preaching? What should preaching be? What does the Church seek to accomplish through preaching? My experience tells me it is not sufficient to merely say preaching is important and must be the central focus of the ministry of the Church. To have an effective preaching ministry requires raising and understanding the questions set forth above.

If preaching is God's tool by which His sheep are fed, how does it relate to the word of God? *The Second Helvetic Confession of 1566* has a very important statement concerning this question:

> Wherefore when this Word of God is now preached in the church by preachers lawfully called, we believe that the very Word of God is preached, and received of the faithful; and that neither any other Word of God is to be feigned, nor to be expected from heaven: and that now the Word itself which is preached is to be regarded, not the minister that preaches; who, although he be evil and a sinner, nevertheless the Word of God abides true and good (Reformed Confessions Harmonized, 1999).

The principle that preaching is the word of God requires the following criteria: it takes place in the context of the public worship of God's people; the preacher is faithful to the Scriptures; and preaching takes place under the oversight of the eldership of the Church.

A key passage in the Scriptures concerning this understanding of preaching is found in Romans 10:14 (the American Standard Version is preferred here): "How then shall they call on him in whom they have not believed? And how shall they believe in him whom they have not heard? And how shall they hear without a preacher" (Romans 10:14)? When properly translated (see Hendriksen, p. 348, footnotes) it is clear that Paul understood that when the gospel is preached, Christ Himself is heard. In his commentary on Romans, John Murray (1959) states it this way: "A striking feature of this clause is that Christ is represented as being heard in the gospel when proclaimed by the sent messengers. The implication is that Christ speaks in the gospel proclamation" (p. 58). This understanding of the text is also supported by the *Expositor's Greek Testament* (1967) when commenting on this text: "It is simplest to render, How are they to believe on Him *Whom* they have not heard? Identifying the voice of the preachers with that of Christ" (p. 673). The evidence points to a very high view of preaching. It is necessary to understand that preaching is Christ speaking to His sheep as spoken of in John 10.

Obviously this view of preaching has some far reaching implications in terms of the authority of preaching. It also has tremendous implications in terms of the effectiveness of preaching in regard to calling the lost and feeding the sheep. If preaching is indeed the word of God it follows that it would be truly effective through the power of the Holy Spirit.

I once preached a sermon entitled "Fried Preacher For Dinner." In a small mid-western rural setting it is often the custom to have fried chicken for dinner on Sundays. So the idea is that when people go to their home after the worship service they would discuss the sermon and criticize the preacher. It would be done from the point of view that one can decide which parts of the sermon were likable and thus accepted and which parts were rejected. The point I sought to make in the sermon was that rejecting any part of the sermon was not to simply reject what the preacher had to say, it was in fact to reject what God had said. That is not to say that God's people should not be like the Bereans and search the Scriptures to see if the message was faithful to the Scriptures. But if it is understood that when the preacher is indeed faithful to the Scriptures and what he is preaching is the Word of God, then one does not personally decide which parts one likes and which parts one does not. Rather in regard to a sermon which is faithful to Scripture, the only acceptable response is "yes Lord." Hendriksen (1981) addresses this issue as well in his commentary on Romans:

> Every person in the audience must be made aware of the fact that when he rejects the preacher who, as a faithful minister of the word, with insight and enthusiasm presents the glad and glorious tidings of salvation in Christ, *then he is rejecting Jesus Christ himself!* (p. 350).

I have heard preachers present information as though what they had to say was perhaps good advice and the recipients might find it useful or perhaps not. Such preaching is sort of like "here is what I think and if it is helpful perhaps you might use it." In such preaching there is no authority. It is merely the opinion of the individual. When there is no authority, there really is no effectiveness in terms of the care of the sheep.

Holding to the notion that preaching is the word of God ought to be very humbling for the preacher. To be in a position of actually delivering God's word to His people can be a very scary thought. What must be kept in mind is that the authority for such preaching actually rests not with the preacher as an individual, rather it rests with the elders in common. The preacher may be the one preparing and delivering the sermon, but the authority is actually in the eldership in common, referred to as "the Spiritual Council" in the RCUS. By extension, this authority is also based in the higher courts of the Church and upon the creeds of the Church. Through my years of preaching I was always very keenly aware of this. If it wasn't for the elders and their oversight and the place of the creeds, it would be impossible to preach with such a concept of authority in preaching. It is a safety net for the preacher to have elders and a creed to guide one on the correct path.

The proper understanding of the authority of preaching will avoid the notion that preaching is simply someone telling others what they ought to do, much as a teenager would label his parents' instruction as "preaching." This then brings together both the concept of authority and the pastoral care for the needy. In his book *The Pastoral Genius of Preaching* (1960) Samuel Volbeda puts it this way:

> The term, "preaching," however, is not to be equated simply with "preachment." As observed above, preaching is the oral communication of that written Word of God to men. Surely, that written Word of God is pastoral through and through in its message, spirit, and purpose. Therefore the spoken proclamation of that pastoral Word calls for an agent who is himself in heart and mind in *perfect harmony* with the pastoral Scriptures which he must preach. He should not be a mere speaking tube or trumpet or phonograph record, reproducing perfectly but mechanically the message of God's written Word. Before one can preach in the true sense of the term, he must have taken up in his heart the message that he must bring and not merely have lodged it in his mind and laid it upon his tongue. He must not merely transmit God's written Word; he must reproduce it in the pregnant sense of that term (p. 26).

As Nourishment for the Believer

Feeding the flock is to provide spiritual nourishment. To nourish someone is to seek and provide for that person's health and growth. At times medicine which does not taste very well and is difficult to swallow must also be provided for someone's health and growth. But the general approach of the shepherd is to take care of the flock, to provide nourishment, to build it up. Covenantal, pastoral ministry must never be to tear down.

Ministry which is dedicated to weeding out the goats from among the sheep or simply to scold the sheep for sin in their lives is not faithful covenantal ministry. While there will always be unbelievers within the Church, ministry is for the people of God. Faithful ministry of feeding the sheep will either convert or expose the unbelievers within the congregation. The congregation must always be seen as the congregation of God's people.

Think again of the beautiful statement in the Heidelberg Catechism Q&A #1 as quoted earlier. The point of this creedal statement is that to belong to Jesus Christ as Savior is to have comfort. That is the covenant assurance: God has made a commitment (covenant) to take care of and feed His people. This serves very well as to what faithful, covenantal ministry is all about. It is to bring this comfort to God's people. It is not to constantly harangue them and cause them to question their salvation. There is way too much ministry that tears down rather than builds up.

Faithful preaching must contain an element of warning; it must call the believer to "work out your own salvation with fear and trembling" (Phil. 2:12). Faithful preaching must even expose the goats which are in with the sheep. Yet such preaching must be within the context of preaching the gospel of good news. It is not the gospel of bad news. The good news is a message of assurance and comfort. I would propose that this is particularly a covenantal theme which begins with God and His promise to His people. To constantly call the people to introspection can lead to constantly doubting as to whether one truly has the hope of eternal life. Every honest individual will find sin in their lives, but the hope of the gospel is that God has provided a covering for that sin in Christ. That again is a message of comfort. The message of the covenant God is one of assurance.

The Goal of Preaching

My Old Testament Professor, Dr. Gerard Van Groningen, taught me a favorite illustration of how to look at a portion or text of Scripture to preach from. To emphasize the pastoral nature of preaching, he referred to all of Scripture as the pasture in which the sheep find their food. A sermon is based on a particular portion, therefore, selecting a text is a matter of fencing off a particular portion of the pasture. The result is that during a particular worship service the sheep are being fed from that portion of the pasture. The message which is proclaimed from that portion is the word of God. The entire Scripture is the word of God, and is food for the sheep, however, a particular sermon is a particular feeding on a particular portion of that pasture. Certainly the specific portion must be placed in its proper context, and there is a place for providing support from other Scripture, but the feeding for the day is from that portion.

In a very real way the goal of preaching and specifically that of a particular sermon is to feed the sheep. That is indeed a very positive concept. In the context of worship, which is to meet face to face with God, preaching ought to result in the worshiper having had a positive experience with God.

Knowing that in preaching Christ Himself is being heard, truly causes the preacher to give serious consideration to what he is engaged in. Preaching cannot be approached as just something to do, with a careless, dull, even boring presentation of facts.

> [P]reaching is actually *heralding, proclaiming.* Genuine preaching, therefore, means that the sermon is lively, not dry; timely, not stale. It is the earnest proclamation of the great news initiated by God. It must never be allowed to deteriorate into an abstract speculation on views merely excogitated by man! (Hendriksen, 1981, p. 350).

The preaching ministry is concerned with lifting up the word of God. There is a strong desire to hold and promote a high view of Scripture. Equally there is a concern to teach the Scripture which is understood to be the trustworthy word of God. There is the conviction that people need to be taught this Word because it is "profitable for teaching, for reproof, for correction, and for training in righteousness, that the man of God may be competent, equipped for every good work" (II Tim. 3:16).

Yet, with such an overall goal for ministry, care must be taken in how we see the role of preaching. When preaching is understood simply to be a teaching opportunity--teaching with detail and precision so that the result is a congregation which has been taught precisely what is in the Bible--then I believe the goal of such preaching becomes distorted. To be sure there is a place and even a necessity for teaching the Bible within the overall ministry to the congregation, but preaching is more and even different than teaching.

Some preachers encourage listeners to take detailed notes while sermons are being preached. I usually do publish a general outline of the sermon in the bulletin as an aid to the listener. But I do have a concern that note-taking should not get in the way of worshiping God. It must be remembered that preaching is in the context of worship. Worship is much more than simply an intellectual exercise.

In preaching, God's word is certainly revealed; God talks to His people. That means information is communicated. The truth of God is learned. But it is so much more than that. At the risk of using language which sounds neo-orthodox, worship is a real encounter with God. It is an experience of what it means to have God talk to you and fellowship with you. While the sermon certainly needs to be kept central, faithful worship requires that all of the elements of worship are important. A proper reflection of this principle should be seen in the sermon itself. We would do well to take heed to the following concern:

> The consequences of making worship primarily about knowledge are both positive and negative in post-Reformation Protestantism. On the positive side, believers are consistently urged to worship in spirit and *in truth.* Ideally, they are led to heart engagement with their God not by sentiment nor by superstition, but by right understanding of his

Word. Such worship protects the church from error and the believer from idolatry.

The negative impact of turning the sanctuary into the lecture hall is training believers to become merely reflective about the gospel in worship and tempting them to believe that right worship is simply about right thought. As a consequence, the worship focus becomes study, accumulating doctrinal knowledge, evaluating the Sermon, and critiquing the doctrinally imprecise. Congregational participation, mutual encouragement, heart engagement, expressions of grief for sin, and joyous thanksgiving may increasingly seem superfluous, or even demeaning. Celebration is dismissed as "charismatic," awe is lost, and sacrament is reduced to remembrance instead of encounter with the presence of the risen Lord. As another has written even the praise can become more about "exhortation to thanksgiving than giving thanks." When this happens, then those whose hearts yearn to respond to God in all the ways his Word describes (and all the ways he has made us to worship) will seek him elsewhere-including those places where truth has been sacrificed to experience (Chapell, 2009, p. 67).

The goal of preaching must be for God's people to know that they have met with God. Having met with God they know that God has spoken to them. They know that God is their comfort. They are refreshed and ready to live before Him until they meet with Him again. It is truly the nourishment which is unto life.

The Need for Communication to Take Place

Preaching is then really about revelation, about God making known the gospel to His people. As God cursed the serpent in Genesis 3:15, He made known to Adam and Eve that life would continue. They heard Him speak; communication took place between God and man. So in preaching today, faithfully based on the inspired word of God, God communicates to His people by the means of preaching. Specifically it can be defined in this way: "preaching is the divine revelation mediated orally by man from God's written word" (Volbeda, 1960, p. 22).

The following elements then are involved in preaching: God has revealed His word through the inspired writers of the Scriptures. Thus we have the inspired word of God in the written Word. God calls men to use that written Word as the basis upon which they speak the word of God. As a result, it is through the preacher that the word of God preached is the orally communicated word of God. That orally communicated Word is heard by God's people.

Even as the prophet Ezekiel was told in chapter 37 to preach to dead, dried up bones, the words he spoke had to be heard--which was made possible by the Holy Spirit--and the dead bones became alive. True communication took place; the Word was spoken and it was heard.

The Heidelberg Catechism also speaks to this point in Q&A #65;

> Since, then, we are made partakers of Christ and all His benefits by faith only, where does this faith come from?
>
> The Holy Spirit works faith in our hearts by the preaching of the Holy Gospel, and confirms it by the use of the holy sacraments (The Three Forms, 2006).

It takes the work of the Holy Spirit for anyone to hear the gospel and come to faith. What the confession says is that this work of the Holy Spirit is by the preaching of the Word of God.

There is a tendency to concentrate on the importance of a sermon being biblical, which all sermons need to be. The notion which is then held is that if the sermon is orthodox and we depend on the sovereign work of the Holy Spirit then we have fulfilled the necessity of God's people being fed by the means of preaching. This is, of course, absolutely true, but I would hold out for a third component. We are not just interested in the Word being proclaimed, we are equally interested in the Word being heard. Communication involves both the Word being spoken and listened to. The reality of the Word being heard begins with the illumination of the Holy Spirit. But to have communication also requires an awareness of the audience. Audiences do not all listen the same way. Often congregations need to be taught to listen to a well put together, content filled sermon. But it takes care and understanding to bring a congregation to be able to listen to such a sermon.

A sermon may be absolutely orthodox, well put together, solidly based on Scripture, but if it is not well delivered many will not hear it. I have seen preachers deliver entire sermons and virtually never make eye contact with the audience, or deliver the sermon in a totally unimpassioned monotone voice. It is my conviction that in such preaching the preacher has not really communicated the word of God to the flock of Christ.

As a minister of the gospel it is easy to become frustrated with the congregation when trying to get through to them what living the Christian life is all about. The preacher may be convinced that he has clearly and repeatedly addressed certain issues of doctrine and life and it appears that there is no change in the life of the congregation. As a result the preaching becomes more and more negative, filled with condemnation and tearing down rather than building up. Certainly at times the preacher needs to deal with serious issues in a serious manner. Sin in the life of the congregation needs to be addressed. The consequences of remaining unresponsive to the word of God must be made quite clear. Yet a ministry which is predominately negative is not pastoral. The preaching of the gospel must be just that--ministry of the Good News.

I have noticed many times that if a minister does not have a pastor's heart--if he does not have the characteristic of being a shepherd to the sheep--then the sheep will not respond. Specifically, they will not hear the Word.

> So too, ministers must be shepherds at heart, in spirit, in their inmost being, if they are to qualify as shepherds in action, specifically if they are to preach. The pastoral function must have its rootage in the pastoral character. Then preaching will not only have a pastoral purpose in a given case and wear a pastoral aspect, but it will be pastoral in its very genius. Then it will be as natural to shepherd the flock of God wisely and well as it is for a tree to produce fruit after its kind. We must beware of the mistake too often made, of thinking that a man wears the preaching office as he wears his preaching frock; that is, around his frame. To be a father and/or a mother one must be constitutionally possessed of vital fertility; those wanting in this respect may be married but they cannot and will never be parents. Ministers must be imitators of God and of Christ and of the apostles and prophets who shepherded the flock because they were shepherds antecedently (Volbeda, 1960, p. 76).

While I have barely touched on all that is involved in preaching, what does become evident even with a very brief treatment of the subject is that preaching is extremely important and it is important that it be done right. Every preacher would do well to remember the statement by the prophet Isaiah concerning those who proclaim the Good News, as quoted by the Apostle Paul in Romans 10: "How beautiful upon the mountains are the feet of him who brings good news, who publishes peace, who brings good news of happiness, who publishes salvation, who says to Zion, 'Your God reigns!'" (Isaiah 52:7).

The beautiful feet are a reference to the fact that the news is important and that it is an occasion for joy. This is the posture which every minister must remember.

If we are to serve God in our ministry of preaching we must respect God, His words and His people, believe that God is going to work through our Christian ministry, and pray that He will do so. To be servants of God and of Christ in our ministry also means that ultimately we are answerable for our ministry to God alone (I Cor. 4:4) (Adam, 1996, p. 127).

Stepping into the pulpit to preach the word of God can never be taken lightly. May God grant to all who would seek to obey God's call to the ministry be constantly aware of the high calling for which God has determined to use faithful preaching.

6

FEEDING THROUGH COVENANTAL INSTRUCTION

The central focus of the pastoral ministry is on preaching. We must guard against any movement away from that focus. This study has also noted the need for pastoral ministry in meeting the needs of individuals. It is important to understand that pastoral ministry involves a teaching aspect. In this study I have argued that preaching is not simply an academic exercise. Therefore, there is a need for instruction in a setting apart from worship. This calls for a type of teaching in which one can thoroughly present the doctrines revealed in Scripture in a detailed, point by point manner and which allows for very specific life application.

Basis for and Historic Practice of a Teaching Ministry

The Apostle Paul exhorted Timothy to provide such teaching to his congregation:

If you put these things before the brothers, you will be a good servant of Christ Jesus, being trained in the words of the faith and of the good doctrine that you have followed. Have nothing to do with irreverent, silly myths. Rather train yourself for godliness; The saying is trustworthy and deserving of full acceptance (I Timothy 4:6-7). For to this end we toil and strive, because we have our hope set on the living God, who is the Savior of all people, especially of those who believe. Command and teach these things (I Tim. 4:9-11). Paul goes on to say in II Timothy 2:24-26:

And the Lord's servant must not be quarrelsome but kind to everyone, able to teach, patiently enduring evil, correcting his opponents with gentleness. God may perhaps grant them repentance leading to a knowledge of the truth, and they may come to their senses and escape from the snare of the devil, after being captured by him to do his will.

In the early church, adult converts were considered to be catechumens and received extensive training, sometimes for as much as six years (Williard, 1852, p. 11). The writing of the Heidelberg catechism, referenced in this study, was intended to provide instruction for both youth and adults so that they would be knowledgeable about their faith. It is a strong tradition in the RCUS to have Sunday school classes for all ages, as well as a number of opportunities for Bible studies. So in addition to the catechization of the youth, there is a commitment to biblical and doctrinal teaching.

The Current Need for a Teaching Ministry

The need for instruction for God's covenant people is greater than ever before. As American Christianity has moved toward an experience-oriented faith, the knowledge of Christian doctrine and of the Scriptures has deteriorated. The move away from the knowledge aspect of faith toward an experience aspect appears to be directly related to a Christian faith that knows less and less about the Scriptures.

But the largest factor in this internal change, I think, was that evangelicalism began to be infected by the culture in which it was living. And then Christianity became increasingly reduced simply to private, internal, therapeutic experience. Its doctrinal form atrophied and then crumbled (Wells, 2008 p. 8).

Surveys have also given strong indication of Christians who are woefully lacking in Biblical knowledge: "The larger scandal is biblical ignorance among Christians. Choose whichever statistic or survey you like, the general pattern is the same. America's Christians know less and less about the Bible (www.christianity.com, Albert Mohler).

The bad news is that religious knowledge in general, *including knowledge of one's own religion*, is abysmal. This includes ignorance of some very basic teachings, and as such, it is obviously a major contributor to the decline of Christianity as the dominant or prevailing worldview that it once was in most Western countries.

This indicates that among other things, the church simply isn't teaching its members basic knowledge about the Bible and Christian doctrine. Forget about complicated topics such as the Trinity as three *hypostases*, one *ousia*; most can't even articulate very basic, different views of communion and soteriology (the doctrine of salvation). The average churchgoer may well be completely ignorant of people like Job and even Abraham and Moses who should be Sunday School staples. This is more clear evidence that the entertainment-driven programs of many churches are clearly not producing people who can articulate even the most basic tenets of their faith, or who know the Bible (Bates and Cosner, 2010).

It may be that churches that have historically been quite faithful in providing a strong Christian education program are not as bad as indicated above. However, we should not assume that members in Reformed churches are immune from this anti-intellectual trend. We also should not assume that, when we receive new members--whether they are new converts or coming from another church--they are well informed concerning Christian doctrine. I believe that in the context of church growth the Church has deliberately attempted to make joining the Church as easy as possible. We would do well to take a lesson from the Church of the first several centuries and require a much more rigorous training program for potential members.

A Model for a Teaching Ministry

So what should a healthy program of educating God's covenant people look like? The Puritan pastor, Richard Baxter, had a great concern for not only the preaching ministry but also the teaching ministry to the people of God. He believed that it was the duty of every pastor to know the people of his congregation personally and to not only preach in a way that truly challenged them in their lives and faith, but also to have a teaching ministry to each member on a personal level.

> In a word, we must teach our people as much as we can of the word and the works of God. What two volumes these become for a minister from which to preach! How great, how excellent, how wonderful, how mysterious! All Christians are disciples or scholars of Christ, and the Church is His School. We are His ushers. The Bible is His textbook. And this is what we should be daily teaching to those in our care (Baxter, 1982, p. 71).

To achieve this, Baxter advocated what he referred to as "personal catechizing" (p. 106). It might be impossible to accomplish the type of "personal catechizing" today which he was able to do in his ministry. But there is certainly a great deal to be learned from his understanding of educating God's people. He saw great benefit in this ministry:

> 1. Personal ministry is a vital advantage for the conversion of many souls. It is necessary that you do personal ministry on a systematic basis. Merely meeting to resolve some controversial issue, or meeting infrequently, would not have the same benefits.

> Personal conversion involves two things: a well-informed judgment of basic issues, and the change of will that is brought about by this truth. Moreover, we have the best opportunity to imprint the truth upon the hearts of men when we can speak to each

one's personal needs. If you have the compassion of Christ, you will exercise this ministry. If you are co-workers with Christ, you will not neglect the souls for whom He died.

2. Personal ministry, when it is well managed, will also build up those being established in the faith. How can you build without laying a good foundation? How can people advance in the truth when they are not first taught the essentials? The fundamental we need to lead men to is further truth (p. 106).

A Specific Program for Christian Education in the Church

In spite of the dumbing down of Christianity referenced above, there is a lot of interest in studying the Bible today. One can find numerous different groups, for example medical doctors, or business men, who meet for Bible studies. There are numerous Bible study aids which can be purchased to assist groups who get together for this purpose. The difficulty is that these studies often purposefully attempt to be without doctrine, and are led by untrained men, or they have no leaders and everyone simply provides their opinion. One wonders if such studies are not more detrimental than helpful.

There is also a very popular movement of establishing small groups within the congregation for Bible study and fellowship. Again the problem is that they are led by untrained men, and are often not for establishing foundation as Baxter advocated but to provide some experience. It is somewhat ironic that while there appears to be a real interest in Bible studies, at the same time Christians are less and less truly informed about Biblical knowledge and doctrine.

I want to once again emphasize that the proposal for a strong teaching ministry should not be seen in any way as taking away from the centrality and importance of the preaching ministry.

I am not advocating something shallow as a means of satisfying those who want to get away from sound preaching. But I am emphasizing the fact that pastoring from a covenantal perspective is more than preaching. I am also committed to the notion that sound preaching must be precept upon precept. Yet in maintaining the unique setting for preaching which is in the context of worshiping God, it seems to be good to have a proper place for both preaching and teaching.

I distinctly recall an occasion when a member of the congregation I was pastoring stated to me that he got more out of my Sunday School lessons than out of my sermons. At first I wasn't sure how to respond to this, but it occurred to me that he was merely reflecting what I believe is the appropriate distinction between preaching and a teaching lesson. Let us remind ourselves of this distinction. Preaching has content which should be informative, but it is also important to remember that it is in the context of worship. The listener is brought directly before God and experiences meeting with Him. In contrast, a Bible study or Sunday School is by nature more of an academic exercise. In a Bible study one can make very precise points in dealing with a matter of doctrine. Certainly in preaching there is an informative word from God going to the listener. But I would not want to merely describe it as an academic exercise.

My exhortation for ministers is to work towards that which the Apostle Paul prayed for concerning the church at Ephesus:

> For this reason, because I have heard of your faith in the Lord Jesus and your love toward all the saints, I do not cease to give thanks for you, remembering you in my prayers, that the God of our Lord Jesus Christ, the Father of glory, may give you the Spirit of wisdom and of revelation in the knowledge of him, having the eyes of your hearts enlightened, that you may know what is the hope to which he has called you, what are the riches of his glorious inheritance in the saints, and what is the immeasurable greatness of his power toward us who believe, according to the

working of his great might that he worked in Christ when he raised him from the dead and seated him at his right hand in the heavenly places, far above all rule and authority and power and dominion, and above every name that is named, not only in this age but also in the one to come (Eph. 1:15-21).

In any program there is always the potential for misuse. There is no one way to carry out an educational program in the church . As mentioned above, in the RCUS there is a strong program of Sunday school for all ages as well as family Bible studies. These are based on the desire to educate the membership and to be faithful to the Word of God to teach His Word to His people. Each individual is responsible to know the Scriptures. Families ought to read the Bible and pray together. Yet there is a place for and a requirement that the Church through its ordained ministry lead the congregation and individuals in their growth in the Lord.

A good program of instruction in the Church can only be God honoring and useful when it is understood in the context of pastoral ministry. It provides for the proper motivation and approach in the care of the flock of Jesus Christ.

> The ministerial work must be carried on prudently and orderly. Milk must go before strong meat; the foundation must be laid before we attempt to raise the superstructure. Children must not be dealt with as men of full stature. Men must be brought into a state of grace, before we can expect from them the works of grace. The work of conversion, and the repentance from dead works, and faith in Christ, must be first and frequently and thoroughly taught. We must not ordinarily go beyond the capacities of our people, nor teach them the perfection, that have not learned the first principles of religion (Baxter, 1656, p. 112).

The teaching aspect of ministry should reflect the pastoral nature of ministry. To truly care for the sheep is to feed them the food which will truly nourish. To force feed deep theology to a new or immature believer is not a ministry of caring because it will not result in growth. The same is true when shallow teaching is provided to mature believers. The goal is to provide that teaching which will provide for the needs of congregations that include members at various stages of Christian growth.

7

CATECHETICAL INSTRUCTION

The RCUS is a creedal church, holding to the Three Forms of Unity, Heidelberg Catechism, Belgic Confession, and Canons of Dort as its doctrinal standards. In this study I have already made a number of references to the Heidelberg Catechism in regards to pastoral ministry. I will now move on to the use of the catechism specifically for the training of the covenant youth. The very purpose for producing the Heidelberg Catechism came out of a pastoral concern.

> Elector Prince Frederick III of the Palatinate had called men of reformed principles to the professorship at the university of Heidelberg, entrusting them with the preparation of a clear, concise and popular statement of the doctrines of salvation in catechetical form--a booklet that could be used by young and old alike in the home, in the church and in the school. The responsible authorship was placed upon two young professors: Casper Olevianus and Zacharius Ursinus (Heidelberg Catechism, 1992).

The Concept of Catechization

The practice of teaching and instilling the basic doctrines of the Christian faith by means of questions and answers is called *catechization* or *catechesis*. Instructing covenant youth by means of the Heidelberg Catechism is a strong tradition in the RCUS. Catechesis is first of all simply a method of teaching.

A catechism from *kata* = "down" + *echein* = "to sound", literally "to sound down" (into the ears), is a summary or exposition of doctrine, traditionally used in catechesis, or Christian religious teaching of Christian children and adult converts, from New Testament times to the present. Catechisms are doctrinal manuals often in the form of questions followed by answers to be memorized, a format that has been used in non-religious or secular contexts as well (Wikipedia.org, catechism).

There were a number of catechisms written during the Reformation. The genius of The Heidelberg Catechism is its very personal statements of faith. By means of learning the catechism the student is not only stating the basics of the Christian faith; he is being led to make it his own confession of faith.

Consider Heidelberg Q&A #59. From questions #24 through #58 the catechism considers and explains the articles in the Apostles' Creed. With the conclusion of that section, #59 then is a very personal question about the catechumen's faith.

"What does it help you now, that you believe all this?

That I am righteous in Christ before God, and an heir of eternal life" (The Three Forms, 2001).

As I have instructed covenant youth over the years I have always emphasized the personal faith aspect as defined and stated above, along with the need to know and understand what faith is based upon. The Heidelberg Catechism itself teaches this concept in Q&A #21:

What is true faith?

True faith is not only a sure knowledge whereby I hold for truth all that God has revealed to us in His word, but also a hearty trust, which the Holy Spirit works in me by the Gospel, that not only to others, but to me also, forgiveness of sins, everlasting righteousness, and salvation are freely given by God, merely of grace, only for the sake of Christ's merits (The Three Forms, 2001).

There is no better way to instill faith in the hearts of covenant youth than by catechesis and there is no better catechism for this purpose than the Heidelberg Catechism.

The use of a catechism to teach Christian doctrine can be found throughout the history of the Church and goes all the way back to the Scriptures. In his letter to the Galatians Paul writes, "Anyone who receives instruction in the word must share all good things with his instructor" (Gal. 6:6). The Greek word for "anyone who receives instruction" is the word *katechoumenos*; one who is catechized. In other words, Paul is talking about a body of Christian doctrine ("catechism") that was taught to them by an officer as an instructor (here the word "catechizer") (www.newcitycatechism.com/intro.php).

This definition and reference to the concept of catechizing in the Scripture itself establishes a very important concept in covenantal ministry. Zacharias Ursinus, one of the authors of the Heidelberg catechism, gives the following lengthy description of catechization and its use in the Church:

> The Greek word *katachasis* is derived from *katacheo*, as *katachismos* is from *katachiso*. Both words, according to their common signification, mean to sound, to resound, to instruct by word of mouth, and to repeat the sayings of another. Katacheo more properly, however, signifies to teach the first principles and rudiments of some particular doctrine. As applied to the doctrine of the church, and as understood when thus used, it means to teach the first principles of the Christian religion, in which sense it occurs in Luke 1. 4. Acts 18. 25. Gal. 6. 6, &c. Hence, catechisation in its most general and comprehensive sense, means the first brief and elementary instruction which is given by word of mouth in relation to the rudiments of any particular doctrine; but, as used by

the church, it signifies a system of instruction relating to the first principles of the Christian religion, designed for the ignorant and unlearned.

The system of catechising, therefore, includes a short, simple, and plain exposition and rehearsal of the Christian doctrine, deduced from the writings of the prophets and apostles, and arranged in the form of questions and answers, adapted to the capacity and comprehension of the ignorant and unlearned; or it is a brief summary of the doctrine of the prophets and apostles, communicated orally to such as are unlearned, which they again are required to repeat.

In the primitive church, those who learned the catechism were called Catechumens; by which it was meant that they were already in the church, and were instructed in the first principles of the Christian religion. There were two classes of these Catechumens. The first were those of adult age, who were converts to Christianity from the Jews and Gentiles, but were not as yet baptized. Persons of this description were first instructed in the catechism, after which they were baptized and admitted to the Lord's Supper. . . . The other class of Catechumens included the small children of the church, or the children of Christian parents. These children, very soon after their birth, were baptized, being regarded as members of the church, and after they had grown a little older they were instructed in the catechism, which having learned, they were confirmed by the laying on of hands and were dismissed from the class of Catechumens, and were then permitted, with those of riper years, to celebrate the Lord's Supper (Ursinus, 1852, p. 10).

The practice of catechizing the covenant youth as part of pastoral ministry is well founded both in Scripture and in the reformed tradition. This ministry begins in the home, by the parents. Psalm 78 powerfully calls on fathers to make known the works of God to their children. In the New Testament setting where we find more of a sense of ministry by the pastor to the congregation, the training of covenant youth ought to clearly be a part of the ministry of the Church.

The Rite of Confirmation

From Ursinus we read that the children of believers having been instructed (catechized) in the faith were "confirmed." No longer being catechumens, after being confirmed they were admitted to the celebration of the Lord's Supper. In my experience, the practice of confirmation is often thought of as a practice which is limited to high liturgical churches such as Roman Catholic and Lutheran.

It is a mistake to think of all confirmation as that which is practiced and understood by the churches mentioned above. There is also a reformed and covenantal understanding and practice of confirmation. The German Reformed tradition has practiced confirmation going back to the Reformation. There are three basic views concerning confirmation which can be summarized as pointed out by Grossmann (1995) in his class notes.

> In Roman Catholic confirmation it is taught that the Bishop (local priests may not confirm) is conferring the Holy Spirit through the laying on of hands and anointing with oil, thus enabling the confirmand to live a good life and so to earn his way to heaven. This is in direct contradiction to the Bible's teaching that Christ is the one who baptizes us with the Holy Spirit (Matt. 3:11), and to the biblical teaching of salvation by grace and not by works (Rom. 3:28).

> Lutheran teaching is that in confirmation the confirmand (person being confirmed) is taking to himself the profession of faith made for him by his "sponsors" at the time of his baptism. This idea in turn grows out of the Lutheran teaching that water

baptism confers spiritual baptism or regeneration, and therefore the baptized child has a potential faith which ought to be confessed for him. This Lutheran teaching ignores and contradicts the biblical teaching that not all baptized or circumcised persons will have true faith.

There is an accepted thought that Confirmation is a way of understanding, (and by practice) that all baptized are saved or will have true faith. That comes from Lutheran and Roman Catholic thinking. It is not inherent within confirmation, that is not to say that some reformed have not seen it that way.

Right from the beginning we see this difference among the children of covenant parents. Adam and Eve produced unbelieving Cain as well as faithful Abel. Abraham was specifically commanded to circumcise Ishmael knowing that he would not be a believer (Gen. 17: 18-19, Cf. verses 13-14). And the apostle Paul clearly distinguishes between believing and unbelieving members of the covenant in Romans 3:1-4.

In contrast with these ideas, Reformed covenant confirmation consists in the profession of an adult faith on the part of covenant youth who have come to a self-conscious age and understanding of the gospel promises of the covenant, and who now declare that they personally embrace these promises for their own salvation. It is called 'confirmation' because in it we acknowledge that God has **confirmed** His promises made to these persons in their baptisms by granting them repentance and faith in His Son.

The confirmand is said to be "confirmed because in confirmation the Church assures the covenant youth that it accepts his or her confession of faith as genuine, even while it recognizes that this faith may have lived for several years in the children's hearts before they reached a maturity consistent with a self-conscious and understanding confession of it.

The reformed emphasis (I would say biblical) is on the fact that these youth are covenant youth. As the catechism says, "they are distinguished from the children of unbelievers". This means a great deal in how they are prepared for living as responsible covenant members.

When the Apostle Peter directed the believers in Acts 2:38-39 to be baptized because the covenant promise belonged to them, he identified three categories of individuals who are to claim this promise: "For the promise is to you and to your children, and to all who are afar off." These three categories are first believers, second their children, and third the afar off; that is those whom God will call who are yet outside of the Church. It is important that the children of believers are not looked upon as those who are outside of the Christian community. It is also important that the children of believers must come to faith. Their faith should not be assumed. They have the privilege of the influence which comes from growing up in a Christian home and they are instructed (catechized) through the Church. They are not converted into Christianity; they are indoctrinated in the Christian faith. The ‚Apostle Paul speaks of the faith of Timothy as a heritage which he received having been taught at the feet of his mother and grandmother (II Tim. 1:3-6).

The concept of confirmation then embraces the covenant promises that our children belong to God, that they are to be raised in such a way so that they will clearly know what it means to belong to God, and that they will publically acknowledge that relationship in the context of the covenant community.

How I wish that we might have kept the custom which, as I have said, existed among the ancient Christians before this mis-born wraith of a sacrament

95

came to birth! Not that it would be a confirmation such as they fancy, which cannot be named without doing injustice to baptism; but a catechizing, in which children or those near adolescence would give an account of their faith before the church. But the best method of catechizing would be to have a manual drafted for this exercise, containing and summarizing in simple manner most of the articles of our religion, on which the whole believers' church ought to agree without controversy. A child of ten would present himself to the church to declare his confession of faith, would be examined in each article, and answer to each; if he were ignorant of anything or insufficiently understood it, he would be taught. Thus, while the church looks on as a witness, he would profess the one true and sincere faith, in which the believing folk with one mind worship the one God.

If this discipline were in effect today, it would certainly arouse some slothful parents, who carelessly neglect the instruction of their children as a matter of no concern to them; for then they could not overlook it without public disgrace. There would be greater agreement in faith among Christian people, and not so many would go untaught and ignorant; some would not be so rashly carried away with new and strange doctrines; in short, all would have some methodical instruction, so to speak, in Christian doctrine (Calvin's Institutes, 1973, bk. 4, ch. 19, art. 13).

Along with catechization, the practice of confirmation is a practice rooted in the history of the Church. Specifically the German Reformed tradition has continued the practice to this day. It is a practice which is consistent in recognizing the unique position that the children of believers hold in the Church, while yet recognizing that they need to be led to faith.

Biblical Basis for Covenant Confirmation

The notion that the children of believers have a unique position in their relationship with God was briefly introduced above in reference to Acts 2:38-39. This is an important implication as we examine the practice of confirmation from a biblical perspective. First it is necessary to examine the unique position of children of believers within the covenant people of God.

The Unique Relationship

When parents present their children for baptism they are claiming this unique position. The *Directory of Worship*, (1998), states:

> In the New Testament no less than in the Old, the children of the faithful, born within the church, have interest in the covenant by virtue of their birth, and right to the seal of it and to the outward privileges of the church (p. 16).

The parents are also publically asked to give a positive answer to the following question: "Do you acknowledge that, although our children are conceived and born in sin and therefore subject to condemnation, they are holy in Christ and, as members of His Church, ought to be baptized?" (Directory of Worship, 1988). In claiming this position regarding the children of believers, it is not assumed that these children are all saved and will come to confess true faith. We read in the Bible of men who rejected God such as Ishmael the son of Abraham; Esau, the son of Isaac; and the wicked sons of Eli. The promises of the covenant were all claimed for them in circumcision, yet they grew up as unbelievers. As children they received the outward blessings of living within the covenant community. The Apostle Paul speaks of this advantage in Romans 3:2, when he says "to them were committed the oracles [literally words] of God." He goes on to say in Romans 9 that "they are not all Israel, who are of Israel." This difference is simply attributed to the fact of election. Not all children of believers are elect. As parents we must be very cognizant of the fact that we do not know who are elect and who are not. Yet as Paul says in verse 6 of Romans 9, "it is not that the word of God has taken no effect." In fact, Psalm 78:5-7 makes it quite clear that making known the word of God by fathers to their children is how they come to "set their hope in God".

God's Promise

"A covenant is a contractual relationship established by authoritative words" (Grossmann, 1992). This formal covenantal relationship spoken of in chapter 3 above includes the children of believers, in that God made a covenant with Abraham and his seed, (Gen. 17). The Apostle Paul affirms the continuation of this covenant in Galatians 3:15-18. In this connection then we must refer again to Acts 2:38-39 where the Apostle Peter commands the baptism of the children of believers based on this promise.

Thus, the Bible teaches that the children of believers today are members of the covenant, both because there is only one covenant of salvation in the Old and New Testaments, and because the New Testament itself declares that God's promises belong to them.

As members of the covenant, the children of believers are also members of the Church. Covenant membership itself implies church membership because in the New Testament the covenant community is the Church. As Paul writes to the church in Philippians 3:3: "For we are the circumcision, which worship God in the spirit, and rejoice in Christ Jesus, and have no confidence in the flesh." Furthermore, Christ received covenant children into His presence and declared "of such is the Kingdom of God" (Matt. 19:14). And what is the Church, but the visible manifestation of God's kingdom on earth? (Grossmann, 1992).

It has always been my practice in the ministry to counsel with parents, particularly with their first child, before they present their child for baptism. Often there is the mistaken notion, which I am convinced comes from the common evangelical non-covenantal theology, that children are viewed as individuals who need to be evangelized and converted as anyone else in the world. The parents see themselves as making a promise to God to make such an attempt. According to I Corinthians 7:14, children of believing parents are to be distinguished from children of unbelievers because they are "holy." Being holy does not mean they are automatically saved, but it does mean that they are set apart by God, distinguished from the children of unbelievers because God has claimed them as His own. In this claim by God, that they belong to Him, is the promise of salvation. Again to claim that God has given a promise of salvation does not mean that God has promised to actually save this child. Rather it means that God has promised to provide a means for the child's salvation, that is, Christ the mediator of the covenant. This is clearly made known to the child in that he/she is raised in the covenant setting by believing parents. "They are to be raised as Christians; are to be taught to know and love their Savior (1 Tim. 1:15), and to live godly lives (as Paul also requires in Eph. 6: 1-4). They are not to be raised as unbelievers in the vain hope that they may someday be converted" (Grossmann, 1992).

Expression of Faith

In addition to the unique position of covenant youth in the Church, we must examine the need to express their faith. Having all of the blessings and privileges of being in this unique covenant relationship does not exempt them from the biblical requirement to exercise true faith. The need for the exercise of true faith is abundantly clear: "whoever believes in the Son has eternal life; whoever does not obey the Son shall not see life, but the wrath of God remains on him" (John 3:36). The privilege of being in the covenant is that God provides many opportunities and incentives to believe the gospel, but no one is saved without believing it.

Think of making a promise to your son or daughter that as long as they do not rebel and remain under your oversight you will, when they have reached age 18, provide a car for them. Thus they have a promise, but they do not yet have the thing promised. They have a responsibility to embrace that promise and thus they will receive it. In the same way when a covenant child who has grown up with all of the privileges of being in the covenant does not express faith in God, but rejects God, then the promise has not failed. They have rejected God and are responsible for that. However, to be just as the children of unbelievers, not having the privileges of the covenant, means they do not even have the opportunity to respond in faith. They would be no better off than the children of unbelievers whose opportunity to respond in faith to God is only by means of evangelism.

Responsibility to Instill Truth

Even as parents claim the promises of the covenant understanding that their children belong to God, they take on the responsibility of instilling in them the truth of God in the promise of salvation. There is a responsibility to respond to the word of God with confession and life. In confirmation the youth publically tell of their faith, confess their faith, and commit to living the Christian life as confessing members of the Church. In this way parents and the Church fulfill their responsibilities to God concerning their children claimed by God.

All believing parents want to see their children express their own faith in Christ. The hope for this must be expressed in teaching them the word of God and leading them to come to that faith.

A Public Confession

True faith calls for an actual statement of faith made in a public manner. Jesus said this about confession in Matthew 10:32: "So everyone who acknowledges me before men, I also will acknowledge before my Father who is in heaven." Also in Romans 10:9-10 the Apostle Paul says, "if you confess with your mouth that Jesus is Lord and believe in your heart that God raised him from the dead, you will be saved. For with the heart one believes and is justified, and with the mouth one confesses and is saved." While believers must always be ready to give "a reason for the hope that is in them," the confession called for appears to be more than a casual statement when asked if one is a believer. It would seem to call for the historic practice of making a confession to the elders in the public gathering of the Church.

Not only is confession (by which one is recognized as a communicant member of the body of Christ) supposed to be public, it ought to be more than a mere brief statement such as "I love Jesus" or "I am a sinner." To confess sins requires some knowledge as to what sins are (Ps. 51). It also requires a turning away from sin; thus an understanding of the life that is followed by the repentant sinner.

While we need not make light of simple statements of faith, there is ample indication in Scripture that confession requires some real understanding of what is confessed. Consider for example the great statement of faith in Hebrews 11. Verse 6 states that "whoever would draw near to God must believe that He exists and that He regards those who see him." A meaningful confession understands something of the awesome nature of God, His deeds and His actions. This requires some maturity and intellectual capacity having studied these things. Biblical confession is much more than a statement about feelings and emotions. It involves some understanding of what it means that Christ has come in the flesh, that He is Lord. It is very easy to say "Christ is Lord," but to understand the implications requires some serious intellectual comprehension.

All of these things together make it clear that the Christian confession is neither to be made nor taken lightly. That is why the elders of the Church are given responsibility for judging the genuineness of each person's confession of faith. In confirmation the confirmand appears before the elders, not to be received into membership, but to be recognized as a responsible member of the covenant communion and qualified to participate at the Lord's Table. But as part of the covenant community the child, whose parents publicly embraced the claims of the covenant promises, now publicly demonstrates what it means to be a member of this fellowship. While the public examination is not a test for qualification of membership, it is a true testimony of the covenantal work of God's grace. It is a great privilege to have this opportunity (Grossmann, 1992).

Confirmation Compared with Profession of Faith

Confirmation implies the responsibility to embrace the promises that the parents claimed at baptism. Making such a confession is not optional for a covenant child. God certainly works differently with every individual, but the notion that a young person raised in the covenant setting simply decides on their own when they feel ready to join the Church is not completely consistent with God's covenant promises claimed by parents at baptism. They are in the Church, and they must be trained and eventually be held accountable for the privileges they received. At times it does need to be recognized that a young person may not be ready at a time normally established by the Church. However, ultimately being responsible to confess faith and being a faithful member of the Church is not optional. In fact, if rebellion persists then eventually church discipline must be applied.

Membership Qualifications

Communicant membership is not about having reached a certain age, or being able to pass a certain test of knowledge. Yet elders are not able to see what is in a young person's heart. But some indication of faith must be evident. It therefore follows that there ought to be a certain course of instruction, and some evidence that the instruction has resulted in a confession which is based on understanding and conviction. I do not believe that the requirement for when a covenant youth is to be confirmed is determined so much by age as it is by completion of the course of study (catechesis). Establishing a schedule by the Church to accomplish this course of study usually does require setting a standard for when covenant youth are to participate in catechism class In most RCUS churches the practice is to begin the process around the fifth grade and then be confirmed in the eighth or ninth grade. But there is flexibility.

The term "profession of faith" may be applied to anyone coming to embrace the gospel. But given the unique status of covenant young people, the term applied to them as they fully and responsibly embrace the gospel is "confirmation." This implies that the promises claimed in infancy are now recognized by the Church as being embraced by the individual. I do not mean to quibble about terminology, so long as it is understood that there is a distinction between training covenant youth and leading someone from outside the Church to faith.

It has been suggested that if the youth are allowed to just make their own decision as to when they believe they are ready to be full confessing members, then they might be more dedicated to being responsible members of the Church. This suggests the idea of someone deciding to "join the Church." That is not covenantal. They are in the Church, and confirmation suggests a responsibility to covenant obligations. That does not mean that it is simply a rote process of just going through the motions.

The Approach Needed in Training

As a pastor I have often told parents that the training of children is not unlike brainwashing them. They are to be raised in such a way that they know nothing else but that they belong to Christ. To insist that a child learn about the gospel can become simply a requirement and thus carried out in such a way that all that is accomplished is simply meeting a requirement. One must be very careful not to fall into such an approach. Nor should we shy away from insisting that our children be trained in the faith. Sometimes children are quite reluctant to eat food which is really good for them. Conscientious parents would insist that the child eat the food for their good health. The same principle can be applied in insisting on feeding the spiritual food which is good for the spiritual health of the child.

A Declaration of Faith

When a covenant youth confesses his or her faith, they are not moving from outside of the Church to being inside of it. They are really being confirmed in their church membership on an adult, responsible level. The evangelized adult, on the other hand, is joining the Church by his or her confession of faith as a result of conversion.

The covenant youth is not confessing a faith that is new to him but is declaring that he has embraced the faith in which he has been brought up. It does not matter when the Holy Spirit placed faith in the covenant youth's heart; if his parents and the Church have done their work responsibly, he has from childhood known the teaching of God's word. But God is the one who has given this faith. He has confirmed the promises of His covenant. By the rite of confirmation the Church is recognizing what God has confirmed by means of the young person's response of faith. By means of the practice of confirmation, the covenant youth is fulfilling a responsibility he has had from the time of his conception in his mother's womb. Responding positively to God's call to repentance and faith is not optional but a responsibility for covenant youth.

Confirmation suggests that the confirmand is and has been, as recognized in baptism, within the covenant and thus a member of the Church. While they too need to have a credible profession of true faith, it is approached from the perspective of a duty and an instruction in who they are rather than an invitation to become something. In confirmation it is God, through His servants in the Church who confirms that the one born and raised in the covenant is confirmed in the covenant. In profession of faith it is God, through His servants in the Church, who receives those who are newly brought into the kingdom of God.

Confirmation as Practiced in the RCUS

The historic practice in the RCUS has been for covenant youth to be catechized by the Church under the direction of the pastor. This is not to take anything away from the responsibility of the parents to instruct their children in the faith. It is a combined effort, to not only instill a basic faith but to teach an informed faith. *The Constitution of the RCUS* (Section IV, Article 192) has established the following criteria for confirmation instruction.

Prepared by the Minister

Every pastor shall carefully prepare the youth in his pastoral charge for communicant membership in the Church by diligently instructing them in the doctrines and duties of the Christian religion. The period of instruction shall, if possible, be so extended that the pupils memorize and are able to recite the entire Heidelberg Catechism before confirmation. The course of instruction shall include catechetical explanation and memorization, Bible history, Bible readings and memorizations, and the study of the books and contents of the Bible, the Belgic Confession of Faith, the Canons of Dort, church history, also the singing and memorization of Psalms, hymns, and Scripture songs (RCUS Constitution, 1997).

Again it is important to understand that this is not some sort of test or requirement for membership. But rather it is a curriculum for preparation by the Church for communicant membership as part of its pastoral ministry.

Demonstration of Understanding

Upon completion of the course of instruction the covenant youth are to demonstrate to the elders and before the congregation their understanding of the gospel and the responsibility of acknowledging Christ as Lord. The historic practice has been that those being confirmed are given something of a public examination in the main areas of instruction as laid out in the criteria listed above.

All covenant youth then are required to attend catechism classes beginning approximately at the time in which they enter into the fifth grade. Their participation in catechism class would continue for four or five years. The qualification for communicant membership is not so much a particular age, rather having completed a certain amount of instruction. Unless they refuse to learn anything or show open rebellion against God they would then be confirmed and be recognized as communicant members of the Church.

Some have advocated that young people should not be confirmed until they are older, perhaps seventeen or eighteen, so that they will be more mature and take their vows more seriously. While there is no magic age, the argument of an older age fails to understand the covenant responsibilities. Clearly young people in their early teens are capable of understanding what the Christian faith is and can make a credible profession of faith. Those who are in the Church are always and at every age to be reminded and held accountable of their responsibilities as covenant members. Being more mature is no guarantee of being more responsible. For a possible lesson plan and materials to use in teaching the Heidelberg Catechism see Appendix B.

One of the unintended consequences of confirmation is to see it as a type of graduation. There is a temptation to think that once the period of catechism instruction has been completed then further learning is no longer necessary. The Church must always struggle with members who are not as faithful or interested in the things of God as they should be. But that is not a question of age.

Method for Instruction

There certainly is a fair amount of leeway for churches to fulfill the requirement for confirmation. It is also the case that any church practice can be misused. There is always a need to address these concerns, and to adjust to what is most useful. The practices in the RCUS have been very helpful for the preparation of covenant youth.

There are also a number of ways in which the process of catechesis can be accomplished. I found that in the course of three to five years of instruction one can take the students through the entire catechism with a thorough learning and instruction on each one. But I also would ask the student to continuously review the memorization of catechism previously learned. Thus by the fourth or fifth year of instruction, asking the students to recite large portions and even the entire catechism is a very reachable goal. For a suggested schedule of how to achieve this goal see Appendix C.

Memorization

The practice of memorizing the catechism has become the most difficult aspect of confirmation to maintain. Again it must be emphasized that having memorized the entire Heidelberg Catechism is not a requirement or test for communicant membership. But memorizing is considered to be an important part of the process of instruction. When something has been memorized, it may not always be totally remembered but the basic truth covered will be instilled in the heart.

The modern education philosophy has abandoned the idea of memorization. In my opinion that has taken away an important tool in the education process. I have had many parents and students as they grew older tell me that just the discipline of having to memorize the catechism has been helpful in their education in general. In the final analysis nothing is really learned until it is memorized. For a more complete discussion on the advantages of memorization see Appendix D.

Often the argument is made that it would be better to memorize Scripture rather than the catechism. Certainly the memorization of Scripture is a good thing to do and should be part of the catechization process. However, when memorizing Scripture it is very easy to take God's word out of context. How many people have memorized John 3:16 and totally misunderstood it because they did not know the context? It is also the case that the catechism contains the whole of the message of the gospel. When one has committed the catechism to memory one has basically committed the word of God to memory.

The responsibility concerning covenant youth is indeed an awesome one. A minister of the Gospel who cares for the sheep will give significant attention to this aspect of his ministry. I have found it to be one of the most rewarding aspects of pastoral ministry.

8

PASTORAL OVERSIGHT BY THE ELDERS

The predominant emphasis in this study is the pastoral work of the ordained minister. However, any treatment of pastoral ministry must include something in regard to the work of the elders. The care which Christ as the Chief Shepherd of the sheep provides for His people is carried out through pastoral ministry of the Church. To a great extent we see this being done by means of the pastor, and in most cases it involves one ordained minister. This is certainly true in the RCUS which holds to what has been historically referred to as the "three office view" (The Constitution, 1997, Art. 15). This view maintains that there are three offices in the Church; minister, elder, and deacon. In looking at the offices of minister and elder, it is important to see that they are equal in authority yet have distinct functions and responsibilities to carry out in terms of ministry. The work of the elders must be one aspect of the overall pastoral ministry of the Church.

In the RCUS the minister or ministers and elected elders of the local church form the Spiritual Council (The Constitution,1997, Art. 70). Often their work involves receiving and dismissing members, examining candidates for confirmation, and dealing with church discipline cases. Yet it is clear that there is an ongoing spiritual care for members which must involve the elders. The elders are in fact held accountable to the Lord for their care:

> Obey your leaders and submit to them, for they are keeping watch over your souls, as those who will have to give an account. Let them do this with joy and

not with groaning, for that would be of no advantage
to you (Heb 13:17).

It is expected that elders have contact with members in some
manner in order to fulfill this responsibility. In the RCUS the
delegate elder to the annual meeting of Classis is asked to give an
account concerning this ministry (The Constitution, 1997, Art. 81.)

Family Visitation

Recently one of the elders with whom I work made contact
with a family who was fairly new in the Church. He was
attempting to arrange a time that he could come to their house for
family visitation. Their first response was "what is family
visitation." They were not familiar with that concept. Family
visitation refers to a long established practice in Reformed
churches by which elders visit families concerning their spiritual
condition. This would be an opportunity to inquire as to how they
are doing in regards to the duties of church membership (The
Constitution, 1997, Section I). It would be an opportunity for them
to raise any issues they might have in the Church or in their walk
with God.

I remember when I was a student in seminary, my faculty
advisor would arrange for the students which he advised to see him
about once every several months. It was his way of checking up
on how we were doing with our academic work as well as our
Christian walk. On the occasion of one such visit as I entered his
office, he stated that it was time for a quarterly "grease job." The
idea was that just as a car needs regular maintenance to run well,
so also believers have a need for a regular check up concerning
their relationship with God.

The concept then of family visitation is a way to provide
this ongoing spiritual maintenance for the members of the Church.
All too often there is the notion that when elders are coming to
visit there must be something wrong. It would seem to me that
such a response fails to see the full implication of being a disciple
of Christ. Belonging to Jesus requires that believers live their lives

in service to him. This Christian walk is filled with pitfalls. It is easy to stumble, to struggle, to become lazy about spending time in the Word of God and in prayer. Everyone needs encouragement. The temptation of our own sinful heart and that of the world is a constant reality. When Paul exhorted the elders concerning their responsibility to the sheep, he reminded them of his own ministry among them. "Remember that for three years I did not cease to warn everyone night and day with tears" (Acts 20:31).

Some churches of a Reformed tradition have in the past had a very rigid program of family visitation. Such a program would simply inform every family, on at least an annual basis, that an elder and pastor or two elders would be visiting on a certain evening. The purpose of the visit was to inquire as to the faithfulness of the family regarding their participation in the life of the congregation.

As with any program, there are always dangers of misuse. My wife, who grew up in a Christian Reformed Church, speaks about the fact that when elders came to visit it was understood that there would be certain specific questions asked and certain answers expected. So for her it became a somewhat meaningless exercise in going through a somewhat canned, precise process. I understand that in some churches now, families are assigned a certain time to come to the Church and meet with an elder. This takes place on a certain evening of the week, each family is assigned a very specific time slot--perhaps 15 minutes--and then on to the next family. It would appear that such a precise program with very specific, predetermined questions can become simply a task to accomplish with very little real pastoral ministry.

The opposite extreme of such a program is that an elder arranges to visit a family and spends over an hour just having a nice friendly visit. His purpose is to avoid going through a canned list of questions, but with the less formal visit it can easily become simply a social visit. Such visits might be useful and even appreciated by the members, but it makes the task of visiting every family on a regular basis a huge undertaking. Elders struggle to carry out such a major program of visitation. Often with such an informal approach, visitation does not get done as often as it should.

In my experience as a pastor in the RCUS, elders often do struggle to fulfill this aspect of their duties. We must be very clear in our understanding what the task of elder is and we should give attention to developing a plan that will fit the congregation and that will work.

Taking Heed

There are a number of verses in Scripture which speak to this aspect of the ministry of the Church, with particular emphasis upon the duties and responsibilities of the elders. Perhaps most informative is Paul's exhortation to the Ephesian elders recorded in Acts 20. Brown (2010) addresses this in his book *Called to Serve*.

> For example, when Paul gave his farewell address to the elders of Ephesus, he first spoke of his ministry among them and then of their responsibility after his departure. Of his own ministry he said, "You know, from the first day that I came to Asia, in what manner I always lived among you…how I kept back nothing that was helpful, but proclaimed it to you and taught you publicly *and from house to house*…(Acts 20:18, 20-emphasis added). Then Paul defended his public and private ("house to house") ministry, saying that he was "innocent of the blood of all men" (v. 26). Why? Because he never shunned proclaiming and declaring the whole counsel of God.
>
> But Paul, headed for Jerusalem, was about to leave them and did not expect to return. So he gave this directive to the elders: "Therefore take heed to yourselves and to all the flock, among which the Holy Spirit has made you overseers, to shepherd the church of God which He purchased with His own blood" (v. 28). Paul in effect is saying, "I shepherded the people while I was with you. I did this in my

public ministry, but also personally and privately ("house"). But now I'm leaving, and you elders need to shepherd the church as I have done" (p. 215).

Kistemaker (1990) points out in his commentary on Acts, that Paul uses agricultural imagery portraying the concept of a shepherd taking care of the sheep entrusted to him. We find similar imagery used by Peter when "He called Jesus the Chief Shepherd under whom elders serve as overseers and shepherds of God's flock." Peter's instructions to fellow elders are particularly informative regarding both the responsibility and task for elders:

> So I exhort the elders among you, as a fellow elder and a witness of the sufferings of Christ, as well as a partaker in the glory that is going to be revealed: shepherd the flock of God that is among you, exercising oversight, not under compulsion, but willingly, as God would have you; not for shameful gain, but eagerly; not domineering over those in your charge, but being examples to the flock. And when the chief Shepherd appears, you will receive the unfading crown of glory (I Peter 5:1-4).

In his commentary on I Peter, Kistemaker (1987) uses the word "pastors" but the concept equally applies to elders:

> Pastors should never forget that they are directly responsible to Jesus, who bears the title *Chief Shepherd* in this text. They ought to remember that the church belongs to Jesus, even though they faithfully love and serve God's people. They must acknowledge that they serve the master Shepherd, whom they serve until he returns. As Jesus' undershepherds, they guide his sheep to the green pastures of his Word and feed them spiritual food (p. 194).

It is common to refer to pastors as "undershepherds." It would be more accurate to refer to pastors and elders as fellow shepherds who carry out the work of the Chief Shepherd. The care of the

113

flock by the elders as shepherds is not secondary to Jesus, but as the shepherds of Jesus, the elders and ministers provide the care of Jesus to the flock.

Another important passage regarding the spiritual oversight of elders is found in Hebrews:

> Obey your leaders and submit to them, for they are keeping watch over your souls, as those who will have to give an account. Let them do this with joy and not with groaning, for that would be of no advantage to you (Heb. 13:17).

This passage underscores the notion that in regard to the care that elders provide for the members, there is an authority structure, there is a task, and there is accountability. And when the members respond there is joy experienced.

> In similar fashion, as a body they are to respond to their leaders, for then there is joy in the interpersonal relationships in the church. They receive the Lord's blessings by obeying the leaders God has given them. If they all respond favorably the work of their leaders becomes increasingly joyful (Kistemaker, 1984, p. 426).

Developing a Plan

I have found it helpful to divide the congregation into groups--sometimes referred to as elder districts--equal to the number of elders. One elder or an elder/deacon team would be assigned to each group. While each elder has responsibilities to the whole congregation, it is much more effective to give elders specific responsibilities to a certain number of members. Here is where it is important to have a sufficient number of elders, so that each will be able to give the appropriate amount of time to their members. Specifically, there should be enough elders so that they are able to visit everyone at least once each year.

Once the members are assigned to the elders a specific plan should be agreed upon in regards to a visitation schedule. This can vary. Some prefer to set aside an evening or two per month and then use the schedule throughout the year. Others may prefer to be more aggressive and accomplish the visitation schedule during a portion of the year. I have found that for the elders to simply agree that they must visit members without a planned schedule does not work very well. The visitation keeps getting postponed. I strongly recommend a specific, workable schedule.

It is also important that the Spiritual Council at its monthly stated meetings receive reports on the visits made and take note of any concerns which have arisen from the visits. In that way the members of the Spiritual Council can hold each other accountable to follow up on the visitation schedule that has been agreed upon.

As preparation for visitation it is also useful for the Spiritual Council to discuss what specific issues might be raised and considered. They might concentrate each year on inquiring about certain areas of the members' spiritual condition. In this way the questions asked and the visit in general would not be seen as some automatic requirement which needs to be fulfilled. If there are some general concerns in the congregation those can be addressed by agreeing to use a specific passage of Scripture to read.

Special Needs

The responsibility to take heed to the flock and to shepherd them requires more than a once per year visit. I believe that a good family visitation program is central for the elders to meet this aspect of pastoral ministry. Yet, it is important to have an ongoing aspect to this work. The elders are not to be domineering by overly checking into the lives of the members. Yet, they need to know the members, be aware of the concerns and difficulties that members are dealing with, and basically come alongside them to care for them. Perhaps most important is to note as to whether their attendance in the public worship is regular. It is often the case that when a certain family begins to be less and less regular in their attendance, there are other issues going on.

There are always members who have ongoing special needs. In such cases extra visits are in order, perhaps just an occasional phone call. Special needs may involve the elderly who are shut-ins. In their case elders might want to make arrangements for more people in the congregation to visit. Shut-ins should feel that they are still members of the congregation. Other needs which require special contact by the elders would be families with a handicapped child, or health issues, etc. In some of these situations it can be useful to get the deacons involved.

Beyond Family Visitation

It would be difficult to measure the benefits of a healthy family visitation program. We must begin with the fact that there is a biblical requirement for the elders to watch over the souls of the members (Heb. 13:17). But clearly the benefits go far beyond. Large churches today use a program referred to as "small groups." While there are practical benefits to small groups, it is not a biblical model. The biblical model is the oversight by the elder. I would suggest that a healthy family visitation program along with the establishment of a specific relationship by elders with members under their care will be a major aspect of community building.

> The Lord provides for his Body in the visiting ministry of the eldership what the secular world tries to duplicate through encounter groups and the like. The confidence, security, and togetherness which can be created by carefully planned and conducted family visiting draws the Church together into the local communion of saints – a communion all seek and one which the secular therapist cannot give (Berghoef & De Koster, 1979, p. 91).

It is very effective to involve elders fairly early in the process of reaching out to new families who have not yet officially joined the Church. As they show interest and begin to go through the process of becoming members, a relationship can already be established between an elder and potential new members. After they have joined it is particularly important to keep close contact and assist them in becoming a part of the congregation. It has been my experience that often conservative Churches are very careful to provide instruction prior to receiving individuals into membership. But as soon as they are members, we sort of leave them on their own. Most need continued instruction, growth, and assistance in getting to the point where they feel at home in the congregation.

Probably one of the biggest frustrations which pastors have in regard to pastoral ministry is when there are specific problems for which members need counseling and the situation has reached a critical point. Often with marriage problems, the couple is about to give up and think about divorce before the minister is aware that there is a problem. If an elder has ongoing close contact, he may be more aware of such situations and able to inform the pastor when appropriate. The sooner problems are addressed the more effective the ministry will be.

9

MINISTRY THROUGH THE COURTS
OF THE CHURCH

The term "church discipline" often conjures up negative thoughts. The Spiritual Council must deal with delinquent or erring members by the process of church discipline. However, properly understood, the concept is broader than that. I remember specifically encouraging someone who was struggling with some temptations in her life. I suggested she needed to join the Church so she could have the advantage of being under the oversight of the elders. She saw that only as a negative because she would then be restrained by their directions. What this individual failed to understand is that as a child of God her best situation would be to follow His direction for life. To truly seek to follow God's direction and to have His blessing is why Christ appointed elders in His church. They provide the guidance that is beneficial for the people of God.

To in fact be under the oversight of the elders is a positive relationship rather than merely a negative one. The reason this is a positive relationship is that not only does the member who places himself under the Church gain by having access to men with wisdom and experience, but also there is the combined wisdom of several elders. The biblical concept of the Church places significant authority in the eldership. They are the voice of Christ to His church. Further, this concept is rooted in the principle that no one elder is to exercise his authority on his own. The wisdom of the elders is the wisdom of many.

The reader may wonder what a discussion concerning church government has to do with pastoral ministry. It is a very important element in pastoral ministry and that failure to use this tool contributes greatly to the failure of pastoral ministry. In this last chapter I will show the useful benefits of making full use of what is called the courts of the Church.

The Concept of Mutual Submission

The term "mutual submission" is used a great deal in the RCUS. It has reference to the fact that in the roles of ministers and elders there is a complete equality of office and authority.

> "Mutual submission" means also what it says. I am in submission to you at the same time you are in submission to me. We function to watch over each other's faith, life and doctrine without either of us having an hierarchical authority (Study 247th Synod, 1995, Part III).

This is particularly true in what is referred to as the courts of the Church. In the local church, Christ's oversight is by means of the Spiritual Council, which is made up of the minister and elders. It is called a court of the Church in that it functions as such. Matters are brought before it to be ruled on. Accusations can be heard, verdicts given, and appeals can be made. In addition to this court with specific jurisdiction in the local church, there is a regional court made up of ministers and one elder from each Church represented in that region. There is also a final court of the entire denomination made up of ministers and elder delegates. In the RCUS these courts are called judicatories, (The Constitution, 1997, Section II).

It is in the functioning of these courts that the concept of mutual submission is applied. Ministers and elders must understand that in the work of the Church they are to be in submission to decisions of the court at each level. This is based on the principle that there is wisdom in numbers and that all, including office bearers in the Church, are sinners subject to wrong thinking and prejudice. It is not only a matter of submission; it is also a matter of welcoming the wisdom of the brethren. To have the wisdom of the brethren is to have a greater, more effective tool in the work of pastoring God's people.

The Authority of Christ in the Courts of the Church

When it is necessary for the court of the Church to actually make a decision and carry out that decision there is an amazing principle involved which is clearly taught in Scripture. This is particularly true when it involves a specific discipline case.

> And I tell you, you are Peter, and on this rock I will build my church, and the gates of hell shall not prevail against it. I will give you the keys of the kingdom of heaven, and whatever you bind on earth shall be bound in heaven, and whatever you loose on earth shall be loosed in heaven, (Mat. 16:18-19).

> Truly, I say to you, whatever you bind on earth shall be bound in heaven, and whatever you loose on earth shall be loosed in heaven. Again I say to you, if two of you agree on earth about anything they ask, it will be done for them by my Father in heaven. For where two or three are gathered in my name, there am I among them, (Matt. 18:18-20).

One might well ask how is it possible that a decision made on earth by less than perfect men can be authoritative and that such a decision is actually followed in heaven. That seems incredible. What if the court of the Church made a mistake? Is Christ actually bound by what humans on earth have decided? That is in fact exactly the authority which is given to the Church. However, there are two very important principles involved.

The first principle speaks to how authoritative decisions are reached. Notice that members of the Spiritual Council are to be "gathered in my name." They are to be totally guided by Christ, seeking the will of Christ which is revealed by His word. Thus the decision must be totally based on what is clearly taught in Scripture. Also there must be agreement amongst two or three. This decision cannot be arrived at by one elder. The wisdom of the plurality of elders must be brought to bear.

The second principle is the process of submitting an appeal to a higher judicatory. If it is thought that the elders at the local level erred, the members of the higher court--Classis or Synod--can be asked to deal with the matter and render a decision. By this process, more learned men with a greater opportunity to truly discern the will of Christ can be brought to bear.

The important thing to keep in mind in this entire process is to see the importance of the concept of mutual submission. Christ is the Chief Shepherd (I Peter 5:1-4) and all of the members of the courts of the Church are His shepherds. They mutually together seek the will of the Lord in the matters of the Church.

Specific Application to Pastoral Ministry

I trust that by now it has become obvious that pastoral ministry is not an easy matter. At times there are really difficult issues which take great discernment and wisdom. Also, at times members are convinced that they have been wronged by the decisions made by the local court.

Occasionally there are issues which involve pastoral ministry and yet do not deal with a specific discipline case. Sometimes there are simply difficult matters which could use the wisdom of more church officers than the local Spiritual Council. These issues can also develop into major conflicts either between the pastor and the Consistory or the pastor and the congregation. All too often congregations suffer great upheaval and members are lost. Sometimes these things are unavoidable, however, every effort should be used to bring a good biblical and pastoral application to the problem. Obviously, when such things occur the spiritual health of the congregation suffers.

The Positive Use of the Courts

The use of the courts of the Church is an important tool in the overall pastoral ministry. It is also my experience that this tool is not used nearly enough. There are probably several reasons for that. I find that the average member is not aware of the options available in seeking to bring matters of serious concern to the attention of the Church beyond the local congregation.

When Spiritual Councils request assistance in carrying out their ministry there can be a sense of failure in admitting that help is needed. This is probably even more true with regard to ministers. It can even become a matter of pride in not wanting to admit that assistance is needed. It can also become a matter of stubbornness. It is easy to become convinced of the correctness of the position taken to the point of being unwilling to have someone else provide advice. But that is not an appropriate approach to take for a minister.

Obviously, the Spiritual Council is responsible and in most cases well able to provide the correct direction for a congregation, to deal with specific discipline issues and to provide proper pastoral oversight. But when these issues do get to the point where there is serious conflict and controversy, the use of the courts can be a very positive thing.

It is difficult to understand the resistance to seek the help of a ruling from a higher court, whether it is a particular case or simply a matter of concern which can truly affect the spiritual life of the congregation. Let us consider the potential outcome. If a pastor has serious disagreement with someone on an issue, and a considerable portion of the congregation is in agreement with that individual, there is only one of two things that can result from taking the matter to a higher court. If the higher court agrees with the pastor then the pastor has that much additional authority and moral persuasion in the congregation. On the other hand, if the higher court does not uphold the pastor's position and determines that he is incorrect, then a good pastor should welcome that because he would not want to be incorrect. Ministers who care for their members ought to be pleased when the higher court of the Church has provided a biblical remedy.

Being a pastor or a member of a Spiritual Council carries with it an awesome responsibility. If one has any sense of being a servant of God--a shepherd serving the Chief Shepherd--the last thing one should want to do is lead the congregation in a way that is incorrect. As a pastor who understands the principle of mutual submission, one should welcome being corrected by the higher court. I strongly encourage pastors to use this avenue when appropriate. The results are only positive and healthy for the Church. It is easy to speak of mutual submission, but it is more difficult to actually put this concept into practice.

Resource for Members

It concerns me that when congregations are struggling, individuals often believe that they are not being fed or that they are being wrongly fed, but they are convinced that they do not have any options. This gets particularly difficult when the elders are all in full support of the pastor and when the pastor is quite domineering. The members then believe they must either put up with the situation or leave and go to a different church. Members need to know that they have other options. Pastors who truly care about their flock will make sure the members are aware of their options as they are spelled out in their church's constitution.

A member may certainly inquire and seek a remedy from the Spiritual Council. When a member does not receive the remedy he is convinced is correct, and when he is convinced that the seriousness of the situation calls for it, the decision of the Council can be complained of or, in the case of a judicial case, appealed to Classis. If necessary and important it can even be appealed to the Synod. Spiritual Councils ought to never be afraid of that. Pastors ought to be ready and willing to assist members so the right solution may be found.

In my experience, even as a student in seminary, there is very little interest among members and even with theologians in studying Ecclesiology--the theology of the Church. If there is an announcement in church that there will be a class on how church government functions, there will be very little interest. Yet I am convinced that most controversies and even heresies which plague the Church are rooted in a poor understanding of church government.

The functioning of the Church should not be seen as merely some required tasks that must be carried out. Rather the Church benefits greatly from a good, properly followed use of the system given in Scripture. Such benefits are not just for a smooth running church in its organization, but also for the spiritual condition of the Church.

Once again we see that ministry is most effective when the concepts of covenantal ministry (God's promise) and pastoral ministry (God's care) for His church are fully appreciated.

10

CONCLUSION

God has called his people to Himself; He has called them out of this world. However, He has not immediately taken them into the New Jerusalem. In His wisdom, God has left them to live in this world though not to be of this world. It is in this state that the Church exists and is in need of nourishment. Pastoral ministry meets this need and provision of nourishment. While the church of Christ is on earth, it is the flock for which Christ is the Good Shepherd.

This is a temporary state. All those called will be with Christ in eternity. Until then they are in the Church. The Church is to be the shining light in the world and is the instrument by which God continues to call His own out of the world. Jesus as the Good Shepherd has provided for the ongoing care, feeding, and growth of the sheep. The instrument to accomplish this is the ministers of the gospel. They are the fellow shepherds by which the sheep receive the ministry of the Good Shepherd.

In carrying out this ministry of the Church there are several basic aspects at work. Most basic is the reality that the ministry of the Church is a ministry to those who are established as the people of God. Ministry to them is first of all not to bring them to faith but to nurture them in the faith and to lead them in glorifying God with their lives. Within this ministry there is obviously a means by which God continues to call people out of darkness, whether it is those who are outwardly in the Church but not converted, or those still out in the world.

I have presented pastoral ministry with the above mentioned concept in mind. The fundamental principle is that the ministry of the Church is indeed pastoral in nature. I have defined pastoral ministry in a number of different categories. In presenting pastoral ministry by means of several different categories there is no attempt to downplay the importance of the preaching ministry. Pastoral ministry is to enhance the preaching ministry.

The proclamation of the word of God by means of preaching must be central to all of ministry. Yet, the very essence of that proclamation is to gather the sheep into the fold and to provide their nourishment. Thus there is application of the preached word in terms of the various aspects of pastoral ministry. This study has attempted to show how this ministry is to be carried out.

Obviously, much of this dissertation reflects what I have come to understand about ministry by simply being involved in ministry. However, there are two areas in which I have come to an even greater appreciation for the richness of the reformed understanding of ministry as it is clearly taught in Scripture.

The first is in the area of worship, and specifically the ministry of the word. I have always, even as a young child, understood that worship was coming into the presence of God and that God spoke to His people. My understanding of this concept has only been strengthened by my study and research. The picture of worship in Hebrews 12 is of specific interest to me. All the implications of actually worshipping by faith in the temple of God made without hands have led me to a greater care in the practice and joy of worship.

I have great concern that worship be understood as a celebration of the resurrection of Christ by which we have new life in Christ. Some may react to this statement as a capitulation to the so called contemporary concept of worship. The opposite is in fact the case. To understand that worship is meeting face to face with God requires that our worship reflect the glory of the creator God. Worship can never be about meeting felt needs but about the glory of God. Yet to come into the presence of God and honor His glory is to understand the reality of eternal life. That must truly be an occasion for celebration. True biblical worship must regain the passion and joy of being blessed with standing before God totally at peace with Him.

This also leads to a renewed and even greater appreciation for the preaching of the word of God. I have a strong passion to promote the idea that in true preaching the people of God are actually hearing Jesus speak to them. He calls His sheep to Himself and they hear and are fed by His word (John 10:15-16). Comprehending the implications of such a view of preaching is very sobering. At the same time, what an awesome reality that it is God who will build His church. To be faithful to the word of God is comforting because it leads to the end that God has intended.

The second area for which this study has caused me to have greater appreciation is one that I have emphasized throughout this study. The covenantal relationship which God has established with His people has profound implications as to how the Church, and ministers in particular, must understand ministry. To understand that God has claimed a people as His precious possession (I Pet. 2:9) and that as His people they have an inheritance which is kept by the power of God (I Pet. 1:3-5) must have a profound implication for the approach to ministry.

Every other religion, and all too often heretical understandings within Christianity, provide a means for man to find God. The biblical faith is one which understands that God has provided a way for God to find man. Ministry is not to assist man in finding God, nor is it to continuously cause man to question whether he has indeed found God. True pastoral ministry is to call man to understand that God has come to Him, and to strengthen the believer in enjoying the blessings of what God has done.

It is obvious that I love the Heidelberg Catechism. This study has only strengthened my appreciation for this great statement of faith which the authors of the Catechism were led by God to pen 450 years ago. It is truly a blessing beyond words to have the heritage of being catechized and now teach and preach with the aid of this creed.

The underlying posture then from which the various aspects of ministry have been presented in this study is that of the covenantal relationship which God has established with His people. This perspective is helpful in understanding who the ministry of the Church is directed to, as well as defining what the ministry is about. God is the God of the entire universe. His message of reconciliation is proclaimed to all. Yet, God's purpose for the revelation of the Gospel is to restore to Himself those whom He has determined from before the foundation of the world to be His special people. God has separated unto Himself His own people. They are His possession, He has purchased them, and thus He cares for them.

The distinctiveness of covenant theology is that salvation is about God. God calls, saves, and keeps His people. The success of ministry is based on this reality. It informs the ministry and it defines what biblical ministry is.

It is my hope that this study will be a useful tool for ministers of the gospel as well as elders. Understanding what pastoral ministry is should also be of interest to all members as they care about the church of Jesus Christ.

APPENDIX A

SAMPLE ORDER OF WORSHIP

Currently we are using the following order of worship at Trinity Reformed RCUS, Sioux Falls, SD. Notice there are two Scripture readings. If the Scripture reading for the sermon is from the New Testament then a corresponding Old Testament passage is also used. If the Scripture reading for the sermon is from the Old Testament then a corresponding New Testament passage is used. Once per month the first reading will be a reading from the Law or a particular application of the law.

I also place brief instructions below the order of worship which informs the congregation as to different aspects of worship. Below are two examples.

Be aware that with the Call to Worship, Salutation, and Invocation we are entering into the presence of God to praise Him and listen to His Word. It is important that everyone considers the implication of meeting with God. As we meet with Him, He speaks to us and we respond to Him.

As we come to worship we come to enter into God's very presence. You are all encouraged to prepare your hearts and minds for this awesome experience. It is important that we provide an atmosphere for all to contemplate coming before the Almighty God.

Preparation for Worship

Announcements
Prelude
Music
Silent Prayer

Entering into God's Presence

*Call To Worship, Salutation, Invocation
*Hymn
Heidelberg Catechism: Lord's Day 33 (pg. 870)
Psalm 40
*Hymn
Pastoral Prayer
*Hymn
Scripture Reading: John 2:1-11
Text: John 2:1-11
Sermon: "Christ Made Known Through Signs"
Prayer followed by Lord's Prayer
Offering/Hymn
*Apostles' Creed (pg. 784)

God Sends His Blessing With His People

*Benediction
*Doxology
*Indicates standing

APPENDIX B

LESSONS FOR TEACHING CATECHISM

It is important to keep in mind that the purpose in teaching the Heidelberg Catechism to the youth is to lead them to faith. Therefore, the approach must be more than merely a memorization of facts. The catechism is such a beautiful and personal expression of faith, it is important as the teacher progresses through the catechism that the steps in faith be emphasized.

I have found that emphasizing the following points is very helpful:

1. Be sure the students understand the three-fold division of the catechism as a progression in faith. Within the divisions there are also important categories, such as explaining the Apostles' Creed, the Sacraments, the Law and the Lord's Prayer.

2. Take advantage of challenging the students in terms of their faith. For example Q&A #59 is a great opportunity to press home what faith means. In speaking of "believing all this" the catechism makes reference to the Apostles' Creed and emphasizes the effect of such belief; namely that one is an "heir of eternal life."

3. Emphasize that the third part, dealing with thankfulness, is a response to salvation. The student needs to see that at this point in the progression his salvation is secure. Thankfulness is what those who are right with God do.

4. Make sure the students understand the meaning of the words.

Appendix C contains a schedule for memorizing the catechism. My practice has been to cover one lesson per week from the workbook which will cover the entire catechism in four years. In addition the student also reviews several Q&A each week with the goal of having the entire catechism memorized with the completion of the four or five year course. As the student recites the review Q&A there should also be a brief review of its teaching.

I have included two sample lessons from the catechism workbook, *Study Helps on the Heidelberg Catechism,* by Norman Jones. This workbook has been very helpful as a tool for catechizing the covenant youth.

The Theme of Comfort

Q1. What is your only comfort in life and in death?

That I, with body and soul, both in life and in death, am not my own, but belong to my faithful Savior Jesus Christ, who with His precious blood has fully satisfied for all my sins, and redeemed me from all the power of the devil; and so preserves me that without the will of my Father in heaven not a hair can fall from my head; indeed, that all things must work together for my salvation.

Wherefore, by His Holy Spirit, He also assures me of eternal life, and makes me heartily willing and ready from now on to live unto Him.

This first question of the Catechism is really a summary of all the questions that follow. We may say that it introduces the great truths which are to be explained more fully in the next 128 questions and answers. This question and answer is a very beautiful statement of the Christian gospel, and we should memorize it so as never to forget it. Notice that the gospel (good news) of salvation is concerned with three great matters: misery, redemption, and gratitude. Our misery is the misery of *sin* (not physical pain): We are guilty of sin, and have corrupt, sinful natures, and are under the awful curse of God. But God has not left us to perish in the misery of sin. Rather, secondly, He has graciously provided redemption (salvation) for us, and this is our *comfort.* Comfort is to have strength, hope, and thankfulness in the midst of trouble. And what is this redemption that gives us so much comfort?

Salvation is being taken by God to Himself, so that we no longer belong to the Devil. Each of the three Persons of the Trinity saves us. The *Father* planned our salvation in every detail; the *Son* purchased our salvation by giving His life for us; the *Holy Spirit* applies the benefits of Christ's work to us, gives us personal assurance of salvation, and makes us willing and ready to live in obedience and love to God.

Your attention is called to the fact that the Catechism is written very *personally*. It constantly speaks of "me," "my," "I," and "our." This does not mean, we repeat, that everyone who reads or memorizes these answers is truly saved and knows the comfort of salvation. No, not at all, for this is a textbook and Bible instruction book only for *believers.*

Are baptized *children* believers? The promise of God made to Abraham and to all Christian parents is that their children are also part of the visible church (see Q74); thus you covenant children are considered as part of the church unless you should turn away from the Lord. Some baptized children of the Church do turn away from Christ, but they are the exception rather than the rule, according to Scripture. May God use His Word, and the instruction of this Catechism, to give you faith and to strengthen your faith.

Questions on Number 1
1. This first question is really a _____ of the whole catechism.
2. The Christian gospel is concerned with three great matters. They are:
a)

_____

b)

_____

c)

_____
3. Sin brings misery, salvation brings _____
What is salvation? _____

_____

4. The Christian's "body and _____both in _____ and in _____ belong to (his) faithful Savior, Jesus Christ."

5. Each of the three Persons of God saves us.

a) The Father _____ our salvation.

b) The Son _____ our salvation.

c) The Holy Spirit _____ our salvation.

6. The Savior's blood (death) does three things for us:

a) it fully_____

b) it _____ me from all the power of the Devil

c) and so _____ me.

7. What does the word "redemption" mean? (See the Glossary)

_____

_____

_____

8. Who assures you that you belong to the Savior and have eternal life?

_____

9. Can you truly say you belong to Christ if you are not willing to live for Him? _ True _ False

10. Baptized young people, even if they do not repent and do not believe and obey Christ, may say truthfully, "I am not my own but belong to my faithful Savior." _ True _ False _ Explain:

_____

_____

_____

11. Write out 1 Corinthians 6:20. _____

_____

_____

The Blessing of a True Faith

Q59. What does it help you now, that you believe all this?

That I am righteous in Christ before God, and an heir of eternal life.

This question provides a bridge or stepping-stone between the great truths of the gospel (the message of salvation), which we learned in the Apostles' Creed, and the great benefit of the gospel—justification by faith—which is taught in questions 59–64. Remember that question 21 taught us the nature of true faith, and question 22 introduced the Apostles' Creed, which tells us what to believe (the content of faith). After the Creed was carefully explained in questions 23–58, we now have the question, "What does it help you now that you believe all this" (all the truth outlined in the Creed)?

The answer is that we receive—through faith in the truth—the great benefit of righteousness and justification by grace alone. The order of the Catechism then is very clear and logical:

1. The Nature of true faith: a certain knowledge and a hearty trust. (Q21)

2. The Content of true faith: the Gospel as outlined in the Creed. (Q22–59)

3. The Benefit of true faith: Justification by grace, through faith alone. (Q60–64)

Here, the benefit of justification is stated briefly, to be explained in detail in the next five questions. We are "righteous in Christ before God," that is, we possess a righteousness (obedience to the Law of God), which is absolutely perfect in God's eyes. This righteousness is given to us by the grace of Christ and received by faith alone. Having this perfect righteousness, we are thus justified by God and made heirs of eternal life—it is ours as a right, never to be taken away. We are justified by God from all sin through the righteousness of Christ, our Redeemer, imputed to us.

Questions on Number 59

1. Question 59 serves as a _____ between the content of true faith and the benefit of true faith, which is

_____

_____

2. There is a definite connection between the Apostles' Creed and the doctrine of justification by faith. _ True _ False
   Explain: _____

3. Question 21 taught us the _____

_____

which is having a

(1)_____

and (2) _____

4. The Apostles' Creed gives us the content of true faith. This means:

___a. it tells us what must be known about Christ in order to be saved

___ b. it was inspired by the Apostles

___ c. it must be recited regularly if one is to be saved

5. A person can be saved by faith in Christ even if he has never heard of the Apostles' Creed. _ True _ False _ *Explain:*

_____

6. Match these statements:

Apostles' Creed   Knowing and trusting Christ

A benefit of faith   Content of true faith

The nature of true faith Justification from all sin

7. Question 59 introduces us to the great truth of justification by faith apart from works. Whose righteousness is given to us by faith?

_____

8. "Righteousness" may be defined as perfect

_____to the_____ of God.

9. Being an "heir of eternal life" means what?

_____

_____

10. Write out Titus 3:7.

_____

_____

APPENDIX C

MEMORIZATION SCHEDULE

The following is a suggested schedule that I drafted for students in catechism class to memorize the Heidelberg catechism. They will cover the entire catechism in four years with a schedule by which they will continuously review. The goal is to have the entire catechism memorized in preparation for confirmation. For those who confirm the youth in the ninth grade, they can use the final year to finalize their study in the message of the catechism as well as the Belgic Confession and Canons of Dort. I have found this type of schedule for assigning memory work to be very useful.

Week	Grade 5	Grade 6	Grade 7	Grade 8
1	#1	#35(1)	#69(18&34)	#99(67-68)
2	#2(1)	#36(2)	#70(19&35)	#100(69-70)
3	#3-4(2)	#37(3-4)	#71(20&36)	#101(71-72)
4	#5(3-4)	#38(5)	#72(21&37)	#102(73-74)
5	#6(5)	#39(6)	#73(22&38-39)	#103(75-76)
6	#7-8(6)	#40(7-8)	#74(24&40)	#104(77-78)
7	#9(7-8)	#41-42(9)	#75(25&41-42)	#105(79-80)
8	#10(9)	#43(10)	#76(26&43)	#106(81-83)
9	#11(10)	#44(11)	#77(27&44)	#107(84-85)
10	#12(11)	#45(12)	#78(28&45)	#108(86-87)
11	#13(12)	#46(13)	#79(29&46)	#109(88-90)
12	#14(13)	#47(14)	#80(30&47)	#110(91-92)
13	#15(14)	#48(15)	#81(31&48)	#111(93-94)
14	#16(15)	#49(16)	#82(32&49)	#112(95-96)
15	#17(16)	#50(17)	#83(33&50)	#113(97-99)
16	#18(17)	#51(18)	#84(17&51)	#114(100-101)
17	#19(18)	#52(19)	#85(18&52)	#115(102-103)

18	#20(19)	#53(20)	#86(19&53)	#116(104-105)
19	#21(20)	#54(21)	#87(20&54)	#117(106-107)
20	#22(21)	#55(22)	#88(21&55)	#118(108-109)
21	#23-24(22)	#56(23-24)	#89(22&56)	#119(110-111)
22	#25(23-24)	#57(25)	#90(23-24&57)	#120(112-113)
23	#26(25)	#58-59(26)	#91(25&58-59)	#121(114-115)
24	#27(26)	#60(27)	#92a(26&60)	#122(116-117)
25	#28(27)	#61(28)	#92b(27&61)	#123(118-119)
26	#29(28)	#62(29)	#93(28&62)	#124(120-121)
27	#30(29)	#63-64(30)	#94(29&63)	#125(122-123)
28	#31(30)	#65(31)	#95(30&64)	#126(124-125)
29	#32(31)	#66(32)	#96-97(31&65)	#127(126)
30	#33-34(32)	#67-68(33)	#98(32-33&66)	#128-129

APPENDIX D

STATEMENT ON CATECHISM MEMORIZATION

This article by R. Scott Clark was originally published in the Presbyterian Banner (August 2003).

WHY WE MEMORIZE THE CATECHISM

Introduction

Both children and parents in Reformed congregations often ask, "Why must we (or our children) memorize the catechism? If they must memorize anything at all, should they not memorize Holy Scripture instead?" These are fair questions, but they rest on dubious premises.

The Purpose

The first premise is that memorization is somehow out of date or a backward practice. Quite to the contrary, in most circumstances (there not being any significant developmental disabilities) memorization is a most valuable skill to teach our children and further, contrary to much modern educational theory it is exactly what they want at a certain stage of their development.

The second premise sounds pious but contains within it a sort of sugarcoated poison since it juxtaposes implicitly the theology and teaching of the church against Scripture. As a matter of fact, we understand our catechism to be a good, sound, and accurate summary of the whole teaching of Scripture. As a matter of history, all heretics quote Scripture. What makes us Reformed is how we understand Scripture and this understanding is summarized in the catechism. This is why we have a catechism.

If we thought that catechism was not biblical, we would not use it and, if anyone can show that the catechism is unbiblical, the church ought to revise it to bring it into conformity with Scripture.

We ought to memorize Scripture, it is the Word of God which he uses to bring our children to faith and by which they grow in that faith and in sanctity, but our children also need a framework in which to understand the Scripture they are learning. So Scripture and catechism memorization go hand-in-glove.

God's Word is full of exhortations to "confess the faith" either by precept or by example. Deuteronomy 6:4 is perhaps the most fundamental biblical confession, "Hear 0' Israel, Yahweh our God, Yahweh is one." This is a confessional formula to be memorized by all Israelites. John 9:22 and Matthew 10:32-33 teach a Christian duty to confess Jesus as Messiah. Exodus 12:26-27 reflects the ancient practice of God's people of catechizing their children in the history of God's saving acts. This catechesis was part of the process of covenant renewal for those who had been initiated into the covenant through circumcision. In I Corinthians 10 (all) the Apostle Paul says that New Covenant Christians continue that pattern with the sacraments of baptism and the Lord's Supper. The Corinthian problem was that they did not regard sufficiently the holiness of the Supper as a feast of covenant renewal nor did they discern the presence of Christ in the Supper by the Holy Spirit.

Following the Apostolic pattern, catechesis of the children of believers (covenant renewal) and new converts has been the universal practice of the Christian church since the earliest days of the church. The pattern of Christian catechesis was to learn the Apostles' Creed; the Lord's Prayer and the Ten Commandments and the Reformation carried on this tradition.

The Plan

The ancient Christian pattern of instruction is summarized by Dorothy Sayers' wonderful essay, "The Lost Tools of Learning," which is widely available in print and on the Internet. In this essay she distinguished the three stages of childhood development as "parrot, pert, poet." Of course, this was her way of explaining the traditional educational pattern of the Trivium, i.e grammar, logic and rhetoric.

In the "parrot" stage (circa ages 4-9), children take great delight in the accomplishment of memorization and are capable of memorizing most anything in small units. In our family we simply divided the longer catechism answers into smaller units until they were learned. I have found in church and at home that if we begin catechizing children (including memorization) at 4-5 they memorize with great joy. To be sure, they do not always understand what they are learning but they don't need to understand everything yet. We are still preparing them to renew the covenant formally before the congregation.

In the "pert" stage (circa ages 9-12), children begin to analyze the raw data which they have memorized. Because they lack emotional maturity, the questions may be expressed rudely (hence "pert"), but in fact questions about the faith show that children are trying to make sense for themselves of what they have been taught. If properly catechized, children now have something interesting to discuss at Sabbath lunch, especially in the pert stage. They will also ask questions just before bed such as, "Daddy, how can God be one in three persons?" This will be a good stimulus for parents to learn the catechism for themselves!

In the "poet" stage (circa ages 12-14), children begin to apprehend that there is more to reality than what they can taste, touch, see, smell and hear They begin to learn how to express themselves more appropriately and to appreciate the finer things in life.

Much more importantly, however, if we begin catechizing our children early enough, by the time they reach this stage, we can expect them to begin to "discern the body" (1 Cor. 11:29), to be ready for profession of faith, to take up the covenant for themselves and to be ready to be fed by Christ's body and blood with Christ's congregation. If we catechize our children early on, by the grace of the Spirit, they are able to develop their powers of doctrinal discernment, which they will certainly need.

The Problems

Covenant children may well object to this plan, but they also object to being taken to the dentist or physician and we do not normally listen to their objections because we know that if we do not take them to the dentist, their teeth will be the worse for it. As important as teeth are, we surely agree that there is much more at stake in catechism instruction. So, when our children object, we tell them, "I know you do not always like memorizing catechism now, but when you are old you will be glad we made you do it;" (this is true! I have visited a good number of old folks who were glad to be able to confess their only comfort in life and in death when all sorts of indignities were being done to them).

Therefore we tell our children "We are Reformed, We confess the Reformed faith and in order to commune in this congregation you too must confess the Reformed faith. Learning the catechism is the best preparation for the Reformed faith. How can you confess something with which you're not intimately familiar?"

There are other things we can do to help our children to take up the covenant for themselves.

The first thing is to reclaim the Sabbath. One of the chief purposes of the Sabbath is Christian instruction of our children. Between morning and evening services the children have all afternoon to learn the catechism and to rest. If families follow this pattern from the start, their children will assume that is the correct thing to do and think it odd that others ignore Christ's command.

Though the dentist might not approve, there is nothing immoral about encouraging young children to accomplish a finite task (e.g. one-half of a longer catechism answer) with the reward of a piece of candy. The Orthodox Presbyterian Church pastor Leonard Coppes wrote some years ago about "candychism." It works because children value the candy as much as a token of accomplishment and parental approval as for the sweet itself. Then, of course, there is the matter of duty. Sometimes it is necessary to use the same sort of approach we use with weekday schoolwork. Learning the faith thoroughly and intimately is a responsibility of a covenant child just as it is his responsibility to learn grammar and math. If they refuse, they should face appropriate discipline. Some parents have even been known to promise a talk with the "board of education." This last resort is effective when used sparingly by parents.

To reluctant Christian parents I ask some questions. Do you want your children to be Reformed when they grow up and if so, how do you expect to achieve this goal apart from the catechism? Why would you by-pass the prime season for catechizing your children?

One of the great losses of failing to catechize children in the "parrot" stage is that in these years children have perhaps the greatest facility for memorization they will ever possess. As we grow older, it becomes progressively more difficult to memorize new material. Any adult who has endeavored to learn a second language knows the truth of this axiom.

Recently I was reading the minutes of a North American ecclesiastical assembly from the early 1920's. Even then, they were establishing a committee to discuss the problem of children leaving the church. Eighty years later, we are still erecting such committees and asking the same question. Perhaps it is time to try something old fashioned? Rather than lamenting the fact that our children are leaving the church, perhaps we should try catechizing them again? As a minister on a Consistory (Session) I am bound to say that if parents will not catechize their children or bring them to church for catechism, they may not blame the church when their children come under discipline fifteen years later because they married a Roman Catholic or left the Christian faith altogether.

Reformed catechesis, however, is not mere obligation. It is a joy and a gift from our covenant Lord. If we do make catechesis a regular part of the religious life of our children, if we make regular use of the ordinary means of grace (Shorter Catechism 88), if we pray and read with our children, we may expect them to make a credible profession of faith in the congregation. Watching our children make profession and come to the table of the Lord, these are the answers to the prayers of all Reformed parents. May God grant us such graces.

BIBLIOGRAPHY

Abstract of the Minutes of the 261st Synod, The Reformed Church In The United States

Adams, Jay. *Preaching With Purpose.* Phillipsburg, NJ: Presbyterian and Reformed Publishing Company, 1982.

Adam, Peter. *Speaking God's Words.* Vancouver, BC: Regent College Publishing, 1996.

Bannerman, James. *The Church of Christ, Vol. I.* Edinburgh, Scotland and Carlisle, PA: The Banner Of Truth Trust, 1960.

Bates, Gary and Cosner, Lita, *Pew survey reveals basic ignorance of Christian belief,* Creation ministries international, www.creation.com/religion-survey-reveals-ignorance-of-bible/.

Baxter, Richard. *The Reformed Pastor.* Edited by William Brown, Carlisle, PA: The Banner Of Truth Trust, 1862.

_____. *The Reformed Pastor.* Abridged and Edited by James M. Houston, Portland, OR, Multnomah Press, 1982, based on editions from 1656 and 1830.

Berghoef, Gerard and De Koster, Lester. *The Elders Handbook.* Grand Rapids, MI: Christian's Library Press, 1979.

Bierma, Lyle D. *The Covenant Theology of Caspar Olevianus.* Grand Rapids, MI: Reformation Heritage Books, 2005.

Bridges, Jerry. *Trusting God.* Colorado Springs, CO: Navpress, 1988.

Brown, Michael, ed. *Called to Serve.* Grandville, MI: Reformed Fellowship, Inc., 2010.

Catechism, http://wikipedia.org/wiki/Catechism/.

Chapell, Bryan. *Christ-Centered Worship.* Grand Rapids, MI: Baker Academic, 2009.

Church Growth Movement, http://www.wikipedia.org/.

Clark, Scott. "Why We Memorize the Catechism" *Presbyterian Banner*, August 2003.

Engle, Paul E. *Discovering The Fullness Of Worship.* Philadelphia, PA: Great Commission Publications, 1978.

_____. "Effective Worship." D. Min. Class Lecture, New Geneva Theological Seminary, Colorado Springs, 2006

Erich, Tom. "Opinion and Commentary." *Aquila Report*, December 2011.

Grossmann, Robert, *Lecture Notes on the Importance of Confirmation.*

Heidelberg Catechism, Green Bay, WI, Reliance Publishing Company, 1972.

Hart, D.G. and Muether, John R. *With Reverence And Awe.* Phillipsburg, NJ: P&R Publishing, 2002.

Hendriksen, William. *New Testament Commentary Exposition of Paul's Epistle to the Romans Vol. II.* Grand Rapids, MI: Baker Book House, 1981.

Horton, Michael. *A Better Way.* Grand Rapids, MI: Baker Books, 2002.

Keil, C. F. and Delitzsch, F. *Commentary on the Old Testament, Vol. 1 The Pentateuch.* Grand Rapids, MI: William B. Eerdmans Publishing Company, 1973.

Keller, Timothy, http://www.newcitycatechism.com/intro.php/.

Kistemaker, Simon J. *New Testament Commentary Exposition of the Acts of the Apostles.* Grand Rapids, MI: Baker Book House, 1990.

_____. *New Testament Commentary Exposition of the Epistle to the Hebrews.* Grand Rapids, MI: Baker Book House, 1984.

_____. *New Testament Commentary Exposition of the Epistles of Peter and of the Epistle of Jude.* Grand Rapids, MI: Baker Book House 1987.

Matto, Ken, http://www.scionofzion.com/decisionism.htm/.

McNeill, John T. ed. *Calvin: Institutes of the Christian Religion.* Philadelphia, PA: The Westminster Press, 1973.

Mohler, Albert, The Scandal of Biblical Illiteracy: It's Our Problem, www.christianity.com/.

Murray, John. *The Epistle To The Romans.* Grand Rapids, MI: Wm. B. Eerdmans Publishing Co., 1959.

Nicoll, Robertson W., ed. *The Expositor's Greek Testament.* Grand Rapids, MI: Wm. B. Eerdmans Publishing Company, 1956.

Old, Hughes Oliphant. *Worship.* Louisville, KY: Westminster John Knox Press, 2002.

Reformed Church in the United States, www.rcus.org,

Robertson, O. Palmer. *The Christ of the Covenants.* Phillipsburg, NJ: Presbyterian and Reformed Publishing Co., 1980.

Schaff, Phillip. *History of the Christian Church, Vol. III.* Grand Rapids, MI: Wm. B. Eerdmans Publishing Co., 1910.

Smallman, Stephen E. *What Is a Reformed Church?* Phillipsburg, NJ: Puritan and Reformed Publishing, 2003.

The Constitution of the Reformed Church in the United States, revised in 1997.

The Directory of Worship For The Reformed Church In The United States, The Synod of the Reformed Church in the United States, United States of America, 1998.

The Holy Bible *English Standard Version,* Wheaton, IL, 2000.

The Reformed Church in the United States, Freeman, SD, Pine Hill Press, Inc., 1975.

The Three Forms of Unity, RCUS, Sioux Falls, SD, Pine Hill Press, 2001.

The View of the Church and its Form of Government as Held by The Reformed Church in the United States, a study commissioned by the 247th Synod of the RCUS, 1995.

Van't Spijker, Willem, ed. *The Church's Book of Comfort.* Grand Rapids, MI: Reformation Heritage Books, 2009.

Wells, David. *The Courage to be Protestant.* Grand Rapids, MI: William B. Eerdmans Publishing Company, 2008.

Williard, Rev. G. W. *Commentary of Dr. Zacharias Ursinus on the Heidelberg Catechism.* Phillipsburg, NJ: Presbyterian and Reformed Publishing Company, 1852.

Witmer, Timothy Z. *The Shepherd Leader.* Phillipsburg, NJ: Puritan & Reformed Publishing, 2010.

Made in the USA
San Bernardino, CA
01 May 2015